POWER HOUSE

A Step-By-Step Guide To Building A Church That Prays

GLEN MARTIN &
DIAN GINTER

BROADMAN
& HOLMAN
PUBLISHERS

Nashville, Tennessee

© 1994
by Broadman & Holman Publishers

4261-44
0-8054-6144-2

Dewey Decimal Classification: 242
Subject Heading: PRAYER // CHURCH RENEWAL
Library of Congress Card Catalog Number: 93-41126
Printed in the United States of America

Scripture quotations marked (NIV) are from the Holy Bible, *New International Version*, copyright © 1978 New York International Bible Society; (NASB) are from the *New American Standard Bible*, © The Lockman Foundation, 1960, 1962, 1963, 1968, 1971, 1972, 1973, 1975, 1977; (TEV) are from *Today's English Version*, New Testament © American Bible Society, 1966, 1971, 1976; and (KJV) from the *King James Version* of the Bible.

Library of Congress Cataloging-in-Publication Data
Ginter, Dian, 1939–
   Power House: a step-by-step guide to building a church that prays / by Dian Ginter and Glen Martin.
        p.   cm.
      ISBN 0-8054-6144-2
      1. Church renewal. 2. Prayer—Christianity. I. Martin, Glen, 1953–.
   II. Title.
BV600.2.G475   1994
262'.001'7—dc20
                                                                    93-41126
                                                                         CIP

We would like to dedicate this work
to Bill and Vonette Bright
for their leadership, encouragement,
and modeling of prayer
to the Body.

Contents

Drawing Closer

First Things First

Prayer power. Most Christians could tell of experiences in which they prayed and God answered, often miraculously. Such experiences are proof to them of the power of prayer. But that is not the kind of evidence a scientist would need to prove prayers are answered and have any impact on circumstances or a person's life. Scientific minds demand controlled experiments, facts, figures, and the like to satisfy their strict set of standards for proof. "But," you may ask, "how on earth would you ever be able to set up such a scientific experiment for prayer? Is it even possible?"

Charles Osgood, veteran CBS reporter and commentator, relates a fascinating story of just such an experiment which was published in *Circulation*. A few years ago Dr. Randolph Byrd, a heart doctor in San Francisco General Medical Center's Coronary Care Unit became curious about the effect of intercessory prayer on patients. He devised a scientifically controlled experiment to see if he could document the effect of prayer on patients. Nearly four hundred patients agreed to participate in a ten-month, double blind experiment. He divided them into two control groups. The article states, "On entry into the study there was no statistical difference between the groups on any of the thirty-four variables. In order to avoid any psychological factors, no one knew whether he was in the "A" group (those being prayed for) or if he was in the "B" group (those in the unprayed for control group).

Pray-ers from across the United States had earlier been contacted and agreed to pray for a person in Group A. The doctor then assigned each to two pray-ers located in different parts of the states. Pray-ers were given only information on the persons' medical problem, not their name.

A San Francisco heart doctor was curious about the effects of intercessory prayer on patients.
▼

After six months of prayer, results were tabulated. Virtually all comparisons were to the advantage of Group A or at least equal to Group B. The following chart shows some of the more significant comparisons between the two groups.

	Group A: prayed for	Group B: not prayed for
tubes needed for breathing or eating:	0	12
antibiotics needed:	3	16
congestive heart failure pneumonia cardiac arrest:	Fewer than B	More than A
pulmonary edema:	6	18

Figure 1[1]

The conclusion drawn by those analyzing the materials was "IP [intercessory prayer] appears to have a beneficial effect in pts [patients] in a CCU [Coronary Care Unit]." Charles Osgood put it this way: "As we used to say about chicken soup: 'it couldn't hurt.'"

A Definite Difference

Glenn Sheppard, founder and president of International Prayer Ministries and current Lausanne Committee traveling prayer representative, has rightly observed this powerful truth: "The more I go and the more places I turn, the more I see that the church that kneels to pray is the church that stands the tallest."

God has shown in many different church settings, the powerful impact prayer can have both to turn impossible situations around, and to expand and accelerate the positive direction of churches already experiencing His blessings. Read the following four stories about churches where prayer has been used of God to accomplish great things.

Champion Forest Baptist Church

Church growth is often illusive, affected by various factors. Many churches try to grab the brass ring of growth and find it just out of reach. However, Pastor Damon Shooks of the Champion Forest Baptist Church in Houston, Texas, is convinced he has found the way his church has been able to capture the "ring" which allowed them to grow from twelve hundred members in 1978 to seven thousand by 1990. "Prayer undergirds everything" he observes.

He has come to realize what many are finding out. The choices: (1) doing things ourselves and struggling to accomplish something for the Lord with all the headaches and problems that can bring; or (2) bringing our needs and problems to the Lord in prayer for Him to meet in a quicker, less traumatic way. This is why Shook can say with such confidence, "when we work, *we* work; but when we pray, *God* works."

The year is 1971. Belmont Church of Nashville, Tennessee, is dying. It has about sixty members, no pastor, and is located in a transitional neighborhood. By all church growth principles, it is doomed. There is much talk about closing down. The situation seems hopeless, but God has other plans. **Belmont Church**

He brings Pastor Don Finto, a man of vision for renewal, a man open to prayer. Because Finto transferred from a local Nashville church, the small group of about twelve who had been meeting with him regularly decided to transfer with him to Belmont. Prayer serves as a strong undergirding for everything at Belmont. This foundation along with a close adherence to the Word and listening to the Spirit's direction are credited for the thirty-five hundred who worship with them weekly in 1993.

Today, prayer saturates all aspects of the church. Every weekday, members gather at the church at 5 A.M. to pray for one hour and beyond about various personal and church concerns. Staff and leadership have weekly prayer times together.

There is a variety of other prayer opportunities such as prayer cells, a weekly intercessory group for children, women gathering to pray for their families and husbands, a group interceding for Israel, people praying during Sunday School and church services for various needs, and missions prayer groups, just to name a few.

Special prayer meetings related to specific causes and concerns of the congregation are frequently called. In addition much teaching is done on prayer, including a yearly special prayer conference with an outside speaker.

It has taken persistence and resisting any attacks of the enemy to discourage them in their praying, but the rewards have been there as they have been willing to push through any roadblocks the enemy tries to erect to stop prayer.

A quarter of a million dollars in debt and only eight members! In 1979 this is what Terry Teykl faced when he accepted the pastoral call to the newly planted Aldersgate United Methodist church in College Station, Texas. Not **Aldersgate United Methodist Church** really the ideal scenario for building a congregation into more than one thousand in weekly attendance by 1993. Teykl confessed, "It was out of desperation that I first began to be really serious about prayer."

The Lord has from the beginning positioned prayer at the heart of all they do. There are many different places and ways for people to be involved in prayer, similar to those mentioned for Belmont. In addition, Aldersgate has prayer at the altar for those who come forward in each service; prayer covering for the staff; a prayer room where members can commit to an hour a week to pray for the church, their schools, government, etc.; a monthly updated prayer list of members and visitors; "Aaronites" who have covenanted to pray one hour a day after being trained by the pastor; weekend prayer vigils; prayer seminars; and prayer for the city to take it back for God. Obviously these many prayer opportunities did not come into existence over night. But down through the years they have expanded from the basics of praying for the survival of and blessings on the church, and the meeting of individual members' needs, to reaching out to the needs of those both in the church and outside its doors.

Teykl sums up their success: "We've learned what Jesus meant when He said, 'My Father's house shall be a house of prayer.' As we've organized prayer, the Holy Spirit has blessed our church in more ways than we can number, but most especially, people have come to Christ and lives have been transformed. Any difficulties or setbacks in mobilizing the church to pray are well worth it to see the Holy Spirit bringing people to Christ. For the sake of the kingdom of God churches need to be on this cutting edge of praying the price."

"The Holy Spirit has blessed our church in more ways than we can number."

▼

Church of Joy

To a large church, prayer can be a wonderful help in accelerating the reaching of its goals. Consider the following. In 1975, a Lutheran church, the Community Church of Joy in Glendale, Arizona, came into existence. By 1989 it had a thriving congregation of around two thousand members. However, by 1992 it had seven thousand members and was adding about two thousand yearly to its membership roles. What caused this influx of people? Did Glendale suddenly have a mass migration of people? No, the pastors attribute much of the growth to the impact of prayer and their taking on a full-time minister of prayer with paid assistant. In addition many volunteers help man the extensive prayer opportunities offered to the congregation.

Today, prayer is such a central focus of their church that it is listed as one of the four church pillars. Prayer requests flood into the church not only from their members but from across the United States and around the world at the rate of more than two thousand a week. They are serious about prayer, and even have a "College of Prayer" which lists ten major areas of study in prayer with fifty-six classes over a year. Their catalog sums up their high view of prayer: "Prayer is not an option for those who want to follow Jesus and be obedient to the will of God. In Matthew 6:5, Jesus says, 'When you pray,' not *if*."

These examples of praying churches are not isolated. Similar accounts could be shared from across the U.S. where prayer has been strategically placed at the heart of a church and has had a significant, even overwhelming, impact.

Prayer: dynamic and exciting or dull and deadly? It will be whatever believers allow God to make it in their lives and that of their churches. It is simple and still complex, natural and yet a skill. Interest in making a church a house of prayer is commendable. Ahead are dynamic principles which will enhance and accelerate the ministry God has given a church. Although the following material in this chapter is aimed at church staffs, lay persons are encouraged to read it, too. There is good information to help strengthen and deepen every prayer life and prepare Christian workers for being used by God to help their churches become powerful houses of prayer.

Dynamic and exciting or dull and deadly—prayer will be whatever you allow God to make it.
▼

Are You Ready?

On the mark. Get set. Go! Are you on the mark? Do you personally have a vibrant, meaningful prayer time? If not, many believers may feel a possible dilemma when thinking, *But my own prayer life is not very good. I just don't have much time to spend in prayer. How on earth am I going to lead the church to become what I am not? I'll feel like a hypocrite!* These are all valid observations of an obstacle to making a church a powerful house of prayer. In part, the answer lies in vision—or a lack of it. Very possibly the reason a Christian does not have time for prayer is very similar to the one a well-known author recently shared. She struggles with not having time for anything but writing. Her story is simple. In fact, she may not have even recognized the truths she shared in a recent writers conference.

"If it's not broke, don't fix it." With a flourish of her hand, a broad smile, and a sense of self-satisfaction, a prominent Christian writer gave her reason for resisting using a computer all these years. Her delivery punctuated the fact that she has no plans to do so in the future. Each year she turns out about twelve hundred pages of typewriter generated

The Deceptive Status Quo

5

materials for her publisher. She was proud of herself, and rightly so for being prolific. "But," as coauthor Dian Ginter relates, "my heart grieved for her as she shared with us the necessity for dedication and probable sacrifices to our writing. She emphasized we might well find, as she has, that we have no time for 'doing' lunch with the girls, shopping, or any of the other fun, relaxing things 'ordinary' people do. Her whole life was portrayed as revolving around her writing."

What this author doesn't realize is that her "cut-and-paste" method of writing, the heavily marked up pages she sends to the publisher, and her many hours of pouring over the typewriter are most likely not producing any higher quality of product or doing it half as quickly as if she were using the computer. For homemade cooking, the extra time is worthwhile. For typing, it definitely is not. In fact, if she would start using the computer, there is a good chance she would see a marked improvement in her end product. She would have more time to refine her writings with much less frustration as she uses her wonderful God-given talent. She might even get to go to lunch with the girls or have some extra, relaxed times with her family.

But to her the unfamiliarity of using a computer, the several hours required to learn computer skills, and the need to leave her comfort zone all probably contribute to keeping her from reaching her full potential in writing *and* living. If she were willing to invest some effort and time, she undoubtedly would certainly reap a high return and reward for her attempt.

Getting on the Fast Track with Prayer

In the same way, not taking advantage of the shortcuts prayer brings to lives and ministry is self-defeating. To go from California to New York, you can get there by any number of means—walking, horseback, car, train, flying, or by the Concord supersonic jet. All will succeed in helping you reach the destination, but you will reach it much sooner with some methods than with others and be able to use the extra time to do other things that are important to you.

Many have not caught the vision that prayer is so crucial; it can actually cut down on the time it takes to do other important things. Martin Luther knew this truth when he said, "I have so much to do today I have to spend four hours in prayer just to get everything done."

Now don't panic! The suggestion is not to spend four hours or even one hour in prayer—well, one would be a great goal. Look more at thirty minutes. Is there willingness to give God—the One you love so much you are willing to go through all that it has taken to be in ministry—1/48th of a day just to talk to Him, get to know Him better, and then find out what instructions He has for the day? But even if you can only give Him ten or fifteen minutes, begin with that and allow Him to increase it as you start enjoying the time with Him more and therefore naturally want to spend more time with Him.

Searching for God

Spending quality time with the Lord inevitably draws believers closer to Him. The following diagram illustrates the way prayer and study of the Word combined can deepen the relationship. Progressing through different levels of relationship with the Lord takes the Christian ever deeper toward His heart and an intimate friendship with Him.

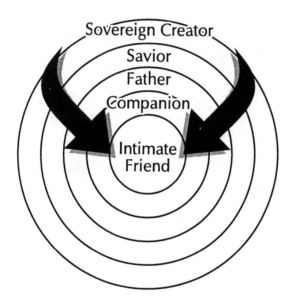

Levels of Relationships with God

Figure 2

God desires a natural progression for all of His children. Many have been successful in going through these levels and reach the very heart of God. David was one who did. He first knew about and believed in God. Then he allowed his knowledge to deepen his relationship with the Lord until he was called "a man after God's own heart." Abraham, too, developed an intimate relationship with God and was called "the friend of God." Enoch's friendship was so close God took him home one day as they fellowshipped.

So how can a level of intimate friendship with God be reached? Although you are not expecting to be carried off to heaven, you should find that once you are saved, the more

The more you get to know the Lord, the more you pray according to His will.

▼

you know about God, the more you learn to trust Him as you see His goodness and power in all areas (Phil. 4:19). As trust grows, commitment naturally strengthens as you get to know and appreciate your loving, caring, giving, omnipotent, omniscient God and Father. You will find Him your constant Companion on whom you lean for everything. Soon an intimate friendship develops with Him. The closer you draw to His heart, the more you are able to sense what He wants and His desires will become your desires.

This closer relationship will return the positive impact on your prayer life. You will find yourself asking for greater things as you pray according to His will, and resist the temptation to go against His will. This releases great power into your activities and helps things go smoother. When problems come, your heart can remain steadier and more focused on the One who will ultimately solve them. As you draw closer to God's heart, you also develop more confidence in Him as to what He can do through you. The deeper your relationship with the Lord, the greater your faith.

When done right, as you go deeper into this relationship, your former perspectives of God will be enhanced. You will have a greater appreciation for His sovereignty, creative abilities, holiness, majesty, etc. For example, James 1:5 says to ask God for wisdom, but warns to ask in faith, since faith comes from knowing God through the Word and prayer. You have a right to ask God to show more of Himself, as Moses did. Faith in a friend comes from knowing him better. Intimacy with a friend never impacts negatively the appreciation of his or her whole nature. It does just the opposite.

David Bryant, founder and president of Concerts of Prayer, recently said it well in paraphrasing Richard Foster in his book *Prayer: Finding the Heart's True Home.* "All prayer boils down to this: You are coming and knocking on the heart of God and He opens the door and He invites you in to explore all the dimensions of His character, of His glory, of His power, of His purposes. And no matter what kind of praying you are talking about, in the end what we are doing is moving deeper into the heart of God."[2]

Different Motivations for Prayer

Moving through the five levels of relationship with God develops differing motivations for prayer. When a Christian knows God only as Sovereign, his or her main motivation usually is to get needs fulfilled. Once a person knows Him as Savior, a high desire to have needs fulfilled still exists. Many will find they are praying about everything. They may also start wanting to pray because they know they should. This later motive becomes a strong motivation when they progress to know Him as Father. There may be a stronger sense of obligation, similar to taking vitamins. They know it will help them spiritually. Many people are stuck at this level of praying. They too often find prayer a chore and difficult to do.

However, as persons broaden the relationship to knowing God as a Companion, time spent in prayer can have the added dimension of wanting to please Him. There is less of a struggle now. The believer who knows God as an intimate Friend finds prayer an exciting thing because he or she *wants* to pray. No longer are they praying to please someone or simply because it is the right thing to do. Prayer flows out from their hearts in a natural, transparent way.

It should be noted that once you reach each new level of relationship, regression is possible if you allow sin or a coldness of heart to set in. But when a deeper level has been reached, the heart will never be satisfied with anything less. This is not to say that at this deeper level the previous relationships will be ignored. As has been mentioned, they will be enhanced and strengthened so you interact with the Lord from all levels, but with only the best of responses.

Another compelling reason to spend significant time with God is that you are in a spiritual battle—we all are. Such time with our Commander-in-chief is needed if we are to be victorious. He waits to meet you, to equip and instruct you for the battle. He wants to let you in on His battle plan so you can win whatever battles your day holds. This can make the difference between a day in which you meet each attack in God's way and one in which your wrong responses have brought defeat to some degree.

Prerequisite for Battle

Don't misunderstand. Just because you spend time in the morning with the Lord is no guarantee your day will be free of problems. But your response and the way you handle these problems will be different. Your mind will be calmer and you will know how to cope with them, dealing with all obstacles successfully, with confidence and a peaceful mind.

Many a believer can testify of the times undesirable responses were averted by meeting with the Lord ahead of time. Sadly, they can also show failures to respond successfully to the enemy's attacks on days where they let time with God get squeezed out by "more important" things. Those are the days they are more vulnerable and may react in anger, in fear, become depressed, be overwhelmed by their circumstances, or may speak an unkind word to someone who is "rubbing them the wrong way." As they go to God with heavy hearts for the day's events, the Holy Spirit would remind them that they were not prepared for that day's battles.

The Wall of Resistance

Knowing a battle is raging leads to another strong factor in your prayer life. When you pray you are engaging in one of the most effective battle strategies the Lord has. So you can expect to meet with strong opposition. It is a wall of resistance you need to push through. Paul makes it clear in Ephesians 6 that believers need the armor of God to live successfully in daily life. In verse 12 he spells it out even more by saying, "we wrestle not against flesh and blood."

When you are thinking about witnessing to someone, you probably find a lot of excuses not to running through your head. *I may offend them. They don't want to hear. Maybe they're not ready. Other people will hear. It is embarrassing to talk about religion. I'm not prepared enough.* Satan will throw anything and everything at you to keep you from witnessing. Often many recognize this and go ahead and witness anyway, pushing through that wall of resistance.

So it must be with prayer. Prayer is so strategic, does so much damage to Satan's kingdom, that he will do *anything* to distract or sidetrack you, intimidate you, including encouraging you to be so busy or feel so tired you will not take the time to pray.

He will give you logical excuses why you should not pray. *I pray all the time. I don't need a special time to pray.* (But Jesus did, and He is God!) *I have so many things to do I don't have time to pray very long.* (We make time for things we know are important.) *Prayer is not one of my strengths.* (If you have a weakness, like a temper, do you work on it or make excuses?) *Prayer is so boring. I find it hard to concentrate.*

Then, too, as church leaders sometimes get so caught up in the theology and business of the Christian life, they unintentionally miss some of the rich relational aspects of walking with the Lord. (Believers can do the same thing with their families, can't they!)

Now these all sound like good excuses not to pray, but in fact they are just that—excuses. In your heart of hearts you most likely know prayer is vital. But in fact it may be a weak area for you, not because you can't but because you've never taken the time to learn how to pray in an effective way.

So ask the Lord right now to help you learn how to increase your prayer skills and to draw closer to Him through prayer. The very fact that you are reading this book indicates you have a desire to have prayer as a potent, effective weapon.

You know He wants you to pray and draw closer to Him. He tells you to pray about everything (Phil. 4:6). Resources 1 and 2 on How to Draw Closer to God and a Two-Week Enrichment program can help you start the process of enriching and expanding your prayer time.

Prayer does so much damage to Satan's kingdom that he will do anything to sidetrack you.

▼

Prayer of Commitment

Pray a prayer similar to this:

> Father, You know my heart. I want to draw closer to You, to be a man/woman of prayer, yet I really don't know how to do so. But I know You do and You want this for me more than I do. So I'm giving You permission to help me pray more—to wake me up early so that I can spend quality, uninterrupted time with You. I covenant to go to bed earlier so I can wake up more alert. When I do get up, help me be wide awake. Show me what I need to do before I start my time with You. Give me a love and an anticipation for this time. Make it so special that I will not want to miss it. Help me draw closer, more deeply in love with You; to trust You more fully; to grow in my confidence in You; to see You truly at work in and through me so that I can be all You created me to be.
>
> Lord, I commit this time to You, now. Make it be a rich one of getting to know You better, of helping me sort through the problems I face, to see Your solutions for them. Use our time together to equip me for this day. Give me a greater love for Your Word and a proper balance in the time I spend in it and in prayer. Feed me, teach me Your truths and cause my roots to be solidly anchored in You and Your Word. Let me be unshakable for You. Keep me pure in all my thoughts, words, and deeds. In every aspect help me keep my flesh under Your control. Teach me to recognize all of the enemy's attacks and then show me how to counter them—with Your Word, with praise, and with prayer.

At the end of your prayer time, close it with putting on the armor of God.

▼

See resources 3A and 3B.

Note: When you pray, you need to do so in faith, believing God will do what you ask. It is His desire and He wants it even more than you do. For example, if you are an evening person and not a morning one, do not allow doubt to inhibit the effectiveness of this prayer. Believe God that He *can* and *will* change You. Walk by faith, not by sight. Just thank Him that He is in the process of changing you, even when you are sleepy. Try showering, doing a few minutes of exercise, drinking something, going out into the cool morning air—whatever it takes to encourage your body to wake up thoroughly. Then have a set place to have your quiet time.

Prayer's Power and Impact

Have you ever wondered why Satan puts up such a fight, resists so hard attempts to pray? Does not this in itself tell how vital prayer is? Would Satan waste his time on something that doesn't matter? No, he's too smart for that. Two strategic things happen while you pray. One, you are drawing closer to God as you get to know and trust Him more. Two, you are engaging in spiritual warfare. You are capturing from the enemy what he has no right to have and helping build the kingdom of God in your church and the lives of all for whom you pray. You will find that the person who draws closer to God and is sensitive to His urging to pray, at times will learn a particular prayer was much more instrumental than he or she was aware of at the time of praying.

Such is the case of an elderly lady in Boston. She went to church one night to hear Dr. Raymond Edmond of Wheaton College. He told of a miraculous death-bed recovery many years earlier when he was a new missionary in Uruguay. "The nationals knew I would die soon, so they had even dug my grave and waited patiently for the time to take my body to be buried. But God had other plans. Unexplainedly I suddenly sat up in bed, asked my wife for my clothes and got up, fully recovered."

When she heard his words, this dear little lady became very excited. After the meeting, she quickly went to talk with him. Upon learning the date of this miracle, she handed Dr. Edmond a very well-worn prayer book and triumphantly pointing to a passage exclaimed, "There it is, you see? At 2:00 A.M. on that date, God said to me, 'Get up and pray. The devil's trying to kill Raymond Edmond in Uruguay!'"

Imagine what the results might have been had this dear lady instead decided that 2:00 A.M. was a better time to sleep than to pray.

Let's Go

It is vitally important to be personally prepared for this strategic step God is asking you to take. All leadership, if not the whole congregation, should try the two-week prayer enrichment program in resource 2. Evaluate it, and if it has been helpful, consider making this your daily routine or incorporating/adapting the helpful elements into your current quiet time format.

So now that you are in the position to be ready yourself, focus on your church. In the next chapter, the emphasis is on what it takes to be a powerful house of prayer. Then, in the following chapters, you can determine where you are in this process. Simple steps are suggested to evaluate your strengths and identify your weaknesses. Powerful tools are recommended which will equip you to give your people a vision so they will become excited and involved in helping your church become a powerful house of prayer.

There are several good books on quiet times in the Annotated Bibliography (resource 4). Also, in chapter 8 under the section "Continue to Draw Closer as Individuals," you will find additional materials which you may want to use at this time. ▼

A Look at Your Future

To give you just a taste of what could happen, stop for a minute. Think about your last difficult board or congregational meeting. What might have been different if more strategic prayer had been added? If a specific team of intercessors, as well as other concerned members and leaders had focused much positive praying on this meeting for the days and weeks preceding it? If there had been a group of intercessors in the audience or a nearby room praying the whole time for the meeting? If the meeting had had a significant time of prayer by the decision makers or leadership expressing the group's desire to have unity and only what the Spirit wanted and that all individuals were willing to lay aside their own interests in order to have the best interests of the whole met?

What would have happened if you were committed to stopping when things started to get difficult or tense and *prayed,* asking the Lord to give fresh insight and control and show His thoughts on the matter? How would this have affected the tone and emotional level of the meeting, the hearts of those participating, the relationships (or lack of it) of those who were not originally in agreement, the future working relationships of the members? These same questions can be applied to any church decision-making body.

Paul said in Ephesians 4:3, "Make every effort to keep the unity of the Spirit through the bond of peace." Prayer was a key part of doing this in the first century. It is just as vital in reaching such unity in the church today. Prayer does change things! It makes a difference when done in the right way. The rewards are great, the effort worthwhile. It is an undertaking that brings many desirable results as you are on the road to becoming a powerful house of prayer. *God is eager and waiting to help your church be all it can be.* So start by understanding what a powerful house of prayer looks like.

▼

Notes

1. Randolph C. Byrd, "Positive Therapeutic Effects of Intercessory Prayer in a Coronary Care Unit Population," *Circulation*, pt. 2, vol. 70, no. 4, abstract no. 845, (October 1984): 212.

2. N-Cup (National Consultation on United Prayer) meeting, Colorado Springs, 1993.

God's Standard

Elements of a Powerful House of Prayer

A well-oiled machine is a joy to behold—intricate parts of all sizes and shapes, close together and yet working smoothly as one. However, the very parts that were designed to work together in perfect, close harmony will tear each other up without proper lubrication. So it is in the church.

Prayer—God's Oil for Relationships

God has provided the wonderful "oil" of prayer, which if properly applied, can help all members work together in spite of the differences. Prayer provides the lubrication so that as a church, made up of different parts, all members can fit together perfectly, working together without friction to perform a job which they could never accomplish on their own.

The same principle is true of the component parts of the church. When heavy duty prayer is applied, the various leadership elements—deacons, trustees, councils, laity, mission groups, etc.—can work in harmony. This means prayer that is enough to saturate the decision-making process, not just a "drop" of prayer at the beginning of a meeting, not just token praying for relationships that do not reach the need, but in-depth praying that not only reaches the needs, but also applies God's oil to the problems, to the points of friction that would otherwise damage or destroy things of value. This really means the whole machine needs oil on an ongoing basis.

Looking further at this illustration, in the world of machinery different kinds of oils—various grades and different weights—are used for a specific need. To apply too light an oil when a heavy duty one is needed can lead to trouble. Too heavy an oil where a light one is called for may gum up the works or be overkill.

The same concept applies to prayer. There are different kinds of prayer for different kinds of situations. God has shown us how to pray for certain results, confess when appropriate, intercede for others, and do spiritual warfare in specific situations. Each fills a need and, when used appropriately, can be the very oil to make our lives and our churches run their best.

The true powerful house of prayer will have prayer saturating every aspect of its life.

▼

A powerful house of prayer is a church that knows the value of the oil of prayer. It is using prayer to maximize all of its ministries and to maintain a smooth running operation. Prayer is acting as a shield against any of the enemy's attacks on all ministries and relationships. This shield of prayer concept will be developed more in chapter 4.

Prayer Ministry vs. House of Prayer

At this point a distinction should be drawn between having a prayer ministry and desiring to be a house of prayer. A prayer ministry involves a portion of the congregation in ministry, as with a youth ministry. A limited number will be involved—usually, those with a greater burden for prayer. Such a ministry may take the form of missionary prayer circles; times of prayer open to the whole church such as a Wednesday night prayer meeting; or men's/women's/youth's prayer meeting; a prayer room; an intercessory team; prayer ministry before/during/after the church service; or a prayer chain. In such cases, prayer will be seen as something done by some but not all of the membership. It will be just another, although important, ministry, as is evangelism or choir.

Some churches have tried to solve this problem by creating a prayer room in their facility, thinking this is the equivalent of becoming a house of prayer. The prayer room can be a very helpful component of the prayer life of a church but should not be the main focus. It is only a part of the overall prayer picture.

All prayer ministries are important for they lay the foundation for becoming a house of prayer since there is already an acknowledgment of the strategic importance of prayer in the church. God will help you build on your current ministry and help you go to the next level of prayer, until you truly become a powerful house of prayer.

So keep up the good work with your prayer ministry, but strive toward the best. Don't let the good become the enemy of the best by being satisfied with where you are. Be willing to board the supersonic jet of a church fully involved in prayer, having a prayer coordinator on staff, and all areas of ministry saturated with strategic prayer. God will help you reach your goal.

The true powerful house of prayer will have prayer saturating every aspect of its individual and corporate life. Having significant prayer will be seen as the first thing to do when planning, when meeting, etc. There will be teaching on prayer from the pulpit, in Sunday School classes, and in small group settings. People will think of prayer as a major factor to be used at first to solve any problem. The whole congregation will be involved in prayer to some degree. Prayer will have a foundational positioning in the life of the individual and the church as a whole.

Why should prayer have a unique position? When prayer is just another ministry or activity offered by the church to interested people, as for example the high school ministry which is aimed at a certain segment of the church, it may handicap the church and its ability to have prayer saturate all areas of the church and congregation. However, when done properly, some churches have been able to use a limited prayer ministry as a stepping stone to becoming a house of prayer. Nevertheless, prayer should be seen much more as a pillar of the church, which if not there or weak will cause the whole structure to be in danger of collapsing. This is a more accurate picture of the reality of prayer in the life of a healthy church. Such a mentality will help a church be on its way to becoming a powerful house of prayer.

The mindset is important. A church may have a prayer ministry but still not be headed toward becoming a powerful house of prayer. In the ideal scenario, everyone is being encouraged to pray and become a part of the prayer ministry in one form or another. In this case having a prayer ministry is appropriate and a necessary step to take for any non-house-of-prayer church.

Prayer Brings Revival

Houston Miles, pastor of Evangel Cathedral, Spartanburg, South Carolina, writes:

> Renewal in our church came in 1971. It was a traditional Pentecostal church named First Assembly of God. It had run the same attendance for about fifteen years prior to my coming, and after 1968, when I took the church, there was still about the same number on Sunday morning—about 175. After three years I was beginning to get discouraged. I wasn't seeing any growth in the church, and I gave serious consideration to quitting the ministry. But I thought that before I did,

I should at least pray about it and wait a while and see what the Lord would do.

On January 1, 1971, I committed myself to prayer. I did everything I could think of to get the people in my church praying. We had prayer cells. We had an around-the-clock prayer chain on Tuesdays. On Sunday I asked for a show of hands: How many would get up thirty minutes early and pray? About 60 percent raised their hands. I organized prayer partners in the church; I instructed the people to get with a partner once a week. "Don't gossip, but pray for the church, pray for the pastor, pray for your own needs." So we prayed for about six months.

Pray, and see what the Lord will do.

▼

The first indication I had that God was doing anything was when people began to come in on Sunday nights. Our crowds on Sunday nights were larger than on Sunday morning, which is unheard of.

From there it just began to explode. We had hundreds of people pouring into our church. We didn't anticipate it—even though we'd been praying for it. The Lord sneaked up on our blind side.

There was no way we could have organized what happened. Before we knew what was going on, the whole thing was just right off the launching pad. There we were with this revival on our hands. It lasted about four months. Almost every night from August to December we had church till about midnight.

After a month or so, I *tried* to close it down. One Sunday night I got up and said, "Well, we've been going about a month now. Everybody's pretty tired. We've been to church every night till midnight. That's enough. Let's close it down." But we came back Wednesday night for the mid-week service, and the place was packed out. We started up every night again!

Looking back on it, I believe we probably could have gone right through 1972. The momentum was there. During those months we saw hundreds of people won to Christ and filled with the Holy Spirit. We saw miracles and healings. We cast out demons.

We have never been the same since. Today we have about twelve hundred people.

If someone asks you to tell them about your church, what is the first thing you bring up? Your great pastor? The inspiring music? The friendly people? Its heart for evangelism? Yours would have to be an extraordinary church for you to mention that it is a praying church, or even have prayer be a third or fourth thing that came to your mind.

That's not to say you don't pray. Everyone does! But it is the rare church that has prayer as a high and visible priority.

When a church is affected by the power of prayer and the presence of the Holy Spirit, it will never be the same. Jesus said, "My house will be called a house of prayer" (Matt. 21:13). Is that what people say about your church? How about the church down the street? Unless you have a most unusual church, you have to say no to that question. Yet, this is both common and the standard for most of the churches across America. Why do they fall short? It is not for lack of desire but rather for lack of instruction and vision.

A House of Prayer Blueprint

This chapter examines nine elements common to churches that are houses of prayer. This examination will help detect both strengths and weaknesses in your local body. That's OK! Just as transformation occurs in the life of individual believers only after they identify the problem, you can also see these transformations are possible in the life of the church as God reveals areas He wants you to address.

The church that is concentrating its efforts on the change agency of prayer makes prayer a part of the solutions offered each Sunday, or shows how it is a vital attribute of the biblical character who is mirroring a way through personal struggles and trials. Paul, writing to Timothy addressing specific leadership qualities essential to his success, shares in 1 Timothy 2:1, "I urge, then, *first of all,* that requests, prayers, intercession and thanksgiving be made for everyone" (emphasis added).

Prayer is visible from the pulpit.

Prayer is a key part of the answer, not something to tack on to the end of a sermon. You can help the congregation appreciate the important part prayer should have in *everything* they do by telling how prayer was a vital part of the lives of Jesus and other biblical characters. Church members can also appreciate the great power for good and change God has given you when prayer becomes an integral part of your own life.

Prayer saturates every aspect of the service. Members have prayed during the previous week for the Sunday services and activities; several pray with the pastor before he speaks and pray during the service; and there are those available after the service to pray with anyone desiring prayer.

Prayers are offered throughout the service.

In a growing house of prayer, all the leadership, staff, and key lay-leaders have a burden and sense of expectancy. They are convinced of its effectiveness and as a way of life, devote significant periods of time to its development in their per-

Leadership is committed to prayer.

sonal lives. This may mean as little as ten minutes or up to an hour or more daily. There is no stipulation as to the "right" amount, only that there is a commitment and follow-through as the Holy Spirit leads you.

Prayer is an agenda item. The prayerful church finds each group meeting, from the leadership and Sunday School classes to the least important board or committee meeting, spending time praying. In addition to significant prayer at the beginning of meetings, when difficulties arise these churches are seen stopping the meetings and seeking the Lord's face for wisdom and guidance and oneness of mind before going any further.

The positive results that happen when this is the practice serve to demonstrate that the church which is a powerful house of prayer has a much lower level of disunity because of the different atmosphere and anticipation as to how God is working, coupled with the desire to seek God's will in all decisions, rather than their own.

Prayer is a part of the Christian education. Periodically, Sunday School classes and/or small groups have a series of teachings on prayer in addition to their regular amount of commitment to praying for the needs of their individual group and other interests. The key is to make prayer a priority in learning and make it meaningful.

Those in any group setting should be trained in several areas of prayer for the small group life. Several ways of increasing prayer follow.

Topical. This kind of prayer is guided by a leader who could be anyone trained to motivate people. In topical prayer the focus can be on one subject or multiple subjects. The group can pray for the church or the government or a specific critical issue in society. The key is the focus.

Conversational. Here, prayer may be random yet concise, focusing on one subject at a time. Anyone can pray for any need, and the group may support that person by agreeing in prayer about the issue that is on their heart. Conversational prayer is brief and is an effective method when prayer requests are not taken. It is less threatening to many.

Applicable. Many times a lesson taught in a class setting has an overriding principle which has touched the listeners hearts in such a way as to make applicable prayer appropriate. Here people are given the opportunity to pray that God's Word and the lesson might continue to impact their lives beyond their study time. Sometimes specific commitments are made about the application.

Expressional. This type of prayer is usually written. People are challenged to write a love letter to God or a note of appreciation for what the Lord has done. One small singles group was instructed to rewrite the Twenty-third Psalm thanking God for His watchcare in their lonely times. This proved to be a very moving experience as the people learned to express their devotion to the Lord.

Transferable. The disciples had the wonderful privilege of seeing prayer modeled by Jesus. One day they approached their Savior and asked to be taught how to pray. Jesus gave them what is called the Lord's Prayer, a transferable prayer by which they could learn the important elements of a successful prayer life. Another transferable kind of prayer is praying the A.C.T.S. way: A, adoration; C, confession; T, thanksgiving; S, supplication.

Meditational. Silence is a powerful tool. Rarely is God allowed simply to speak to hearts because a long shopping list needs to be completed. Occasionally people should just close their eyes and listen. They need to reflect upon how God has been working in their lives and their commitment to His will. Meditational prayer is often very difficult due to our media oriented environment, but it can be a great tool to broaden a person's prayer life and add to it a new dimension.

Relational. In this kind of atmosphere, people are brought together in pairs or triads to pray for one another's needs and hurts. Relational prayer is both valuable and a wonderful time for bonding to occur. Here opportunities are given to open up and reveal the "real you" so that help can be ministered to the pain.

In Exodus 17 a significant event in the life of Israel is revealed. It is also a good model for a powerful house of prayer:

> The pastor has a strong prayer covering.

> The Amalekites came and attacked the Israelites at Rephidim. Moses said to Joshua, "Choose some of our men and go out to fight the Amalekites. Tomorrow I will stand on top of the hill with the staff of God in my hands." So Joshua fought the Amalekites as Moses had ordered, and Moses, Aaron, and Hur went to the top of the hill. As long as Moses held up his hands, the Israelites were winning, but whenever he lowered his hands, the Amalekites were winning. When Moses' hands grew tired, they took a stone and put it under him and he sat on it. Aaron and Hur held his hands up—one on one side, one on the other side—so that his hands remained steady till sunset. So Joshua overcame the Amalekite army with the sword. Moses built an altar and called it The Lord is my Banner. He said,

"For hands were lifted up to the throne of the Lord" (vv. 8–13, 15–16).

Leadership needs prayer support for several reasons.

First, leaders always come under attack. Satan seems to watch for the best time to attack which often is right after a significant victory or when a leader is tired.

Second, even godly leaders cannot win the battle alone. Joshua was to choose men who would go and fight the Amalekites. Any battle worth fighting calls for more resources than the leader possesses by himself.

Third, godly leaders will motivate other people. Moses climbed to the top of the hill for two reasons—insight and inspiration. He gained greater insight when he could see the people, and the people were motivated when they could see him. People often imitate what they see. They need to see leaders praying *and* leaders being prayed for.

Fourth, godly leaders have weaknesses. Moses' arms did grow weary even though his desire was to keep them stretched toward heaven. It is vital for a leader to have Aarons and Hurs available to "lift his arms," recognizing that this produces victory. Prayer teams should be organized that pray daily for the pastor; specifically for the morning worship services and even during the worship services; for the physical, emotional, intellectual, and spiritual life of their shepherd and his family, and for protection over him, his family and possessions, as well as protection of his reputation.

Leadership can be a lonely place, but it need not be an isolated place. Church members can come alongside their leaders, symbolically lifting up their hands through prayers, helping the leader do all that God has called him to do.

Prayer is the first step, not the last resort. In a house of prayer church it is natural to see people praying together about personal problems and interests. Prayer will always be the obvious first step in finding the solution to any situation, and thus pray-ers will be available after services for those who have specific needs that may need addressing. There may even be a designated prayer room for those who desire the confidentiality or need a longer prayer time.

Intercession is an integral part of the church life. In a praying church, a variety of times and places are available for people to gather to pray—early morning, evening, church, homes, even restaurants over a meal, at a business, or with other business people in the area. A strong and efficient prayer chain is in place to serve the congregation's emergency needs and a mechanism whereby the people can communicate the answers to those specific prayer requests. Prayer will be more than an inward look. It will become a dynamic, powerful, and tangible way of influencing the city, the state, the government, the world, helping them come into alignment with God's principles and for His glory.

As a church becomes excited about prayer and their growing and developing prayer skills, they will seek more direction. A director of prayer can hold yearly seminars and develop ministries that impact the local body and create a greater sense of awareness as to the need for more prayer. Increasingly, the church seen as reaching its community will have prayer as a paid staff position.

Larger churches have a director of prayer ministries.

Another feature, though not a necessity, will be a prayer room where various kinds of prayer requests may be found, and people can come to pray for these and other needs.

Developing a powerful house of prayer is no easy task. But then again, success never comes easily. Most successful people are mavericks whose minds roam outside traditional ways of thinking. Instead of trying to refine old formulas, they invent new ones.

When Jean-Claude Killy made the French National Ski Team in the early 1960s, he was prepared to work harder than anyone else to be the best. At the crack of dawn, he would run up the slopes with his skis on, an unbelievably grueling activity. In the evening he would lift weights, run, sprint—anything to get an edge.

But the other team members were working just as hard and long as he was. He realized instinctively that simply training harder would never be enough. Killy then began challenging the basic theories of racing technique. Each week he would try something different to see if he could find a better, faster way down the mountain.

Innovations require a willingness to question the way things have been done.

His experiments resulted in a new style that was almost exactly opposite to the accepted technique of the time. It involved skiing with his legs apart (not together) for better balance and sitting back (not forward) on the skis when he came to a turn. He also used ski poles in an unorthodox way—to propel himself as he skied. The explosive new style helped cut Killy's racing times dramatically. In 1966 and 1967 he captured virtually every major skiing trophy. The next year he won three gold medals in the Winter Olympics, a record in ski racing that has never been topped.

Killy learned an important secret shared by many creative people: innovations don't require genius, just a willingness to question the way things have always been done. It is this very creativity and innovation that must be embraced if prayer is going to be a priority in the church of the nineties and communicate the gospel effectively to our world. Jesus spoke of the gospel as "new wine" that could not be contained in "old wineskins."

Marketing researcher George Barna tells us that unless we are willing to analyze and re-evaluate our Christian traditions and methods—holding on to the relevant and effective and discarding the outdated and ineffective—we will be seriously handicapped in our efforts to reach today's lost.[1] So break the traditional mold of prayer, become "radical" and aim at becoming exactly what your Lord set as a standard for you by becoming a powerful house of prayer. To help you analyze where you are in your journey toward this goal, the next chapter will allow you, through a series of thirty questions, to identify what type of church you are in today: promising, progressing, productive, or powerful.

Notes

1. For an expanded understanding of this point, read all of, but especially chapter 16, *User Friendly Churches,* George Barna (Regal Books: Ventura, Calif., 1991).

3

Evaluating a Church's Readiness

A group of scientists, according to a story by Harold Bredesen, decided to develop a fish that could live outside of water. So, selecting some healthy red herring, they bred and crossbred, hormoned and chromosomed, until they produced a fish that could exist out of water.

But the project director wasn't satisfied. He suspected that though the fish had learned to live on dry land, it still had a secret desire for water.

"Re-educate it," he said. "Change its very desires." Again they went to work, this time retraining even the strongest reflexes. The result? A fish that would rather die than get wet. Even humidity filled this new fish with dread.

The director, proud of his triumph, took the fish on tour. Accidentally, according to official reports, the fish fell into a lake. It sank to the bottom, eyes and gills clamped shut, afraid to move lest it become wetter. Of course, it dared not breathe; every instinct said no. Yet breathe it must.

So the fish drew a tentative gill full. Its eyes bulged. It breathed again and flicked a fin. It breathed a third time and wiggled with delight. Then it darted away. The fish had discovered water!

With that same wonder, men and women conditioned by a world that rejects God live like fish out of water until they discover Him and the remarkable ability to commune and communicate with Him in prayer. In Him you live, move, and have your being. In a vital relationship with Him, you can find purpose for your life, seek His direction, and find comfort and encouragement in the most difficult of times.

The problem in many churches lies in the fact that few in leadership demonstrate such a relationship and therefore are

Men and women have been conditioned by a world that rejects God.

▼

unable to motivate others to reach a deeper commitment to the Lord in prayer. Too few are in a situation to guide their flock to becoming a house of prayer without outside help. An honest examination and evaluation may be appropriate for these churches.

God's Potential for the Church Can Be Blocked

Understanding the dynamics in the flow of prayer may help in recognizing the problem and its solution. The following diagram is a good illustration of what can happen in the life of an individual or a church when there is sin, a lack of desire for prayer, or an absence of skill in how to pray.

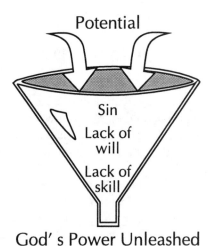

Prayer needs an open "funnel" for God's power to be able to flow through you. If sin of *any size or source* is present, it will block the flow.

Too often it is thought that the little sins don't matter. You (or your church) are no worse than anyone else. What has been forgotten is God's statement in Psalm 66:18, "If I regard sin in my heart, the Lord will not hear me" (KJV). Notice He does not say what size of sin. Any sin qualifies as a sin that will close down God's ability to "hear" us. Isaiah (59:2) reinforces this when he declares, "Your sins have hidden His face from you so He will not hear" (KJV).

Sin has the most potential for blocking God's power, but a weak desire to pray—"lack of will"—and/or a lack of skill in knowing much about prayer will also clog the works and impede God's potential for both the individual and the church. Chapter 4 gives you some steps to take to correct any of these problems.

The Church's Personality

To be able to take the necessary steps to become a powerful house of prayer, you need to determine where you are as a church and thus what type of church you are. A simple tool for such an evaluation follows. Other methods could be used for such an evaluation, but for our purposes we have developed a series of thirty questions divided under the headings of *will* and *skill*, designed to pinpoint a church's weaknesses and strengths. Take a few minutes to answer each question, realizing that the more honest you are in your evaluation, the sharper the needs and direction can be focused.

Evaluating Your Church's Will

	YES	NO
More than 25 percent of our membership is involved in some form of church sponsored prayer activity each week (small group, missions, early morning).	☐	☐
Prayer is frequently mentioned from the pulpit as a solution to the problem under consideration.	☐	☐
Staff/leadership have regularly scheduled prayer times (could be part of another meeting) to pray for each other, church, and congregational needs.	☐	☐
Our church has prayer as a vital ingredient for outreach.	☐	☐
An emergency prayer chain is in place.	☐	☐
The pastor and key leadership are committed to putting prayer in a visible place in all church ministries.	☐	☐
There is a growing interest for continuing education in the area of prayer.	☐	☐
There are various prayer opportunities other than the traditional mid-week prayer meeting.	☐	☐
We have a prayer team in place that prays during the worship service.	☐	☐
People are praying for each other at unscheduled times.	☐	☐
We have a paid staff position for our prayer ministry.	☐	☐
Often all of the congregation has an opportunity to pray for others during the church service.	☐	☐
Overall, when there is a major decision to be made, prayer is a key ingredient to the process.	☐	☐
We have a prayer room which is used frequently.	☐	☐
We have a way of letting people know about answered prayer.	☐	☐

YES	NO	Evaluating Your Church's Skill
☐	☐	The church has a volunteer/staff prayer coordinator who can model various prayer skills.
☐	☐	We have one or more persons who are capable of dealing with people under spiritual attack.
☐	☐	We have had a seminar or some form of continuing education on prayer in the past year.
☐	☐	There is a systematic way of compiling prayer requests and praying for them.
☐	☐	Pastor(s) has (have) a group of prayer partners committed to covering him (them) and their family in prayer.
☐	☐	Our church has identified and is using at least one person with a heart for intercession.
☐	☐	Our people are not afraid to use the term "spiritual warfare" to identify the attacks of the enemy on the ministry and individuals.
☐	☐	We offer opportunities for people to pray with staff or a prayer team at the conclusion of services.
☐	☐	Our members regularly pray with other believers outside of just our own congregation.
☐	☐	We have committed prayer warriors in our congregation who are providing a real prayer covering for all church ministries.
☐	☐	Prayer is seen as the first step in the solution to any problem either within the church or on a personal basis.
☐	☐	Our church regularly sponsors prayer opportunities and prayer teachings for believers from the community.
☐	☐	Teaching articles on prayer appear regularly in our church newsletter.
☐	☐	Our people are excited about prayer and what they are seeing God do in their lives as a result of prayer.
☐	☐	Our members know and are comfortable using several different styles of praying. (See resource 9.)

Count up only the yes answers and put the number in the blanks below.

Will _____   Skill _____

On the next graph plot out the yes totals on the will and skill axis. By connecting the two points, you will discover what category your church is in with regards to its readiness to become a powerful house of prayer. The quiz and chart are not meant to be an exact science. They are only tools to help you get a handle on where you are and where you need to go. These guidelines are flexible even between the categories—thus the dotted lines instead of solid. But the important thing is that you start somewhere and move toward the goal of all churches—that of becoming a powerful house of prayer.

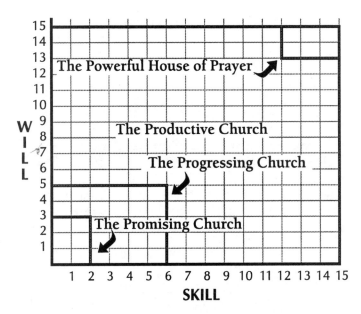

Now that you have identified where you are as a church, consider what your next steps should be. All churches will be going through the steps in chapter 4. Some of these steps may already be a part of your church's prayer life. If so, go on to the next step. For some of you, especially the productive and powerful churches, there may be only a need to bring up to speed members who have yet to put into practice some of these steps in their own life or ministry.

All churches will undoubtedly find they have a mix of people—some with many skills, some with few, if any. These people can be brought up to your current level by using the materials presented from chapter 4 and any other chapters preceding the one specifically targeting your church type.

The following is an overview of the four types of churches.

- The Promising Church. This type of church has minimal prayer ministry and little exposure to prayer training.

- The Progressing Church. This type of church has had vital prayer times in the past but is not praying much now.

- The Productive Church. This type of church has many people with a burden to pray but not a lot of exposure to differing prayer styles.

- The Powerful Church. This type of church has prayer at the heart of everything it does. It is truly a powerful house of prayer.

Five Reminders for All Churches

O.K. You've identified your church type and have a thumbnail sketch of the classification you are in. However, do not be overly pessimistic or draw wrong conclusions from the category in which you find yourself. So here are five things to keep in mind now and as you work through the steps to becoming a powerful house of prayer.

Don't make comparisons. If you do, then you will either run the risk of pride when you see you are doing better than another church, or you will become discouraged if you're doing worse. God has established you as a unique church. He has a special plan for you as a congregation that will help you become a powerful house of prayer. Praise Him for bringing you to where you are, and let Him help you get to where He wants you to be.

Don't be afraid to establish goals. Goals are absolutely necessary. They help keep track of where you are as well as give you direction. But avoid two common mistakes in goal setting: the first is setting goals *too low* ("We will know we are a house of prayer when five people see us this way"); secondly, setting goals that are to be reached *too soon* ("We will be a house of prayer within the next six months"). Setting unrealistic goals is opening yourself up to discouragement and failure. Both can kill the momentum you will have been experiencing. The enemy uses discouragement in prayer as a key way of making people want to give up. There are several things to remember when establishing goals:

- Your commitment as a pastor to the process may be influenced by how long you plan to be at this particular church. You will probably want to be there long enough to see such a program well established and able to continue on without you if you plan on leaving—a two- or three-year minimum would be required. Depending on where you are when you start, this does not mean you would be finished by the time you leave. Yet you should be well enough grounded that the staff, leadership, and laity would be sufficiently motivated to carry it through to completion.

- Be unified as leadership before you approach the church. You may first need to bring the leadership on board and up to speed. Knowing how much the enemy does not want to see effective prayer in the church, you can be certain that unity will be essential to the success of reaching your goals. When the whole leadership is enthusiastic and unified in presenting change, the congregation can catch the vision much quicker and share their enthusiasm.

- Target the whole church, not just part of it. Once your leadership is unified, you can move on to challenging the *whole* congregation. One reason you need everyone can be seen in the illustration of an older city involved in a renovation plan. It doesn't want to leave any unrepaired, rundown shacks alongside the renovated buildings. In the same way, everyone needs to be involved in helping make the church a house of prayer, since the church is made up of individuals who are part of the "building blocks" of the church.

- From start to finish, pray much about your goals and the process. As leadership, take time to seek the Lord for how He wants you to proceed, what steps to take next, which ones to modify or eliminate, and changes in order, additions, etc. Remember, this is a *model* for you to *adapt*. Each church is unique and has a strategy God has specifically designed for you. Let these pages serve as stimuli, resources, and catalysts in finding His precise will and direction for you in prayer.

- Evaluate periodically how things are going. Any good sea captain will tell you that you need to make minor course adjustments at times if you are going to reach your destination safely.

Feel a little overwhelmed? A little excited? That is good! The Spirit has most likely been preparing you and your church for a long time. He is ready to lead you through each step to becoming a powerful house of prayer. If you've looked ahead any, you may feel like the little boy on his first day of school looking at the many years of education it will take to become a doctor. He may get panicky. That is what the enemy would like to happen to you as you start this prayer adventure. But remember, don't look at the obstacles. Look at the Lord and each *single* step. Most are easy to take. All should produce measurable results.

Prepare yourselves for an experience you'll never match with any other church activity. The church that comes alive with prayer is a dynamic, powerful church in all areas of ministry. It *will* accomplish all God has for it. And the road to reaching God's purposes will be much easier when prayer has gone before, smoothing out many of the otherwise rough places.

Recognize the great rewards you will get.

Your church is where it is. You will continue to progress or regress at the same rate unless something intervenes. Therefore, be encouraged that prayer is available to help ensure that progress will be the direction you go. But more than that, prayer will only enhance what the Spirit is already doing in all areas of your ministry. He can use it to speed up the process for you and remove many difficult roadblocks. Remember, anything worth doing takes effort. You never get physically in shape without effort. Neither does a church reach its maximum health by coasting along. Effort is always a requirement along with a significant time investment. The Scriptures paint clear pictures of sacrifice, diligence, and struggles—but coming out on the other side victoriously when done God's way.

The enemy will try to discourage you, but choose not to allow yourselves to get your eyes off the prize God has for you—becoming a powerful house of prayer! And be sure to note the progress you are making as you go. This will serve as an encouragement and increase your desire to press on toward your goal.

Don't listen to the enemy's lies.

The last thing Satan wants is a praying people. He will do everything possible to intimidate and discourage you, to make you feel overwhelmed by the task. He will try such things as telling the pastor he is too weak in his own prayer life ever to be able to lead the church in significant prayer steps—"You will be a hypocrite," or "You can't do this. It is too hard." (See pp. 7–11 for steps to take to enhance and strengthen your own prayer life.)

If you tried to preach only on those things you no longer have a problem with, you probably would have very few sermons. But the truth is that we are all on this journey together. Leaders do not have to be miles out in front of the congregation to lead successfully. (Fortunately, in the pastorate we have learned our sermons are usually meant for us first. We have to process the material through our own lives before we can then give it to our congregation.) Thus, with prayer, leaders can direct members where God is first leading them. And the Lord will be walking by your side, guiding step by step. In such a situation, you may have the exciting opportunity to be truly walking by faith, not by sight.

"How long?" or "We may never reach the goal." The enemy will try to discourage you by saying this is too long, too difficult a process. Resist such thoughts. Instead, recognize that each step your congregation takes toward becoming a powerful house of prayer will be a strengthening step. No matter how long the process takes, you will be going from strength to strength. You will be seeing fruit along the way. Excitement will be increasing and the rewards of the hard work will be many. Since prayer should be an integral part of all your church does until the Lord returns, you can know your efforts are well worthwhile. Knowing this is Jesus' will also should be an encouragement, since when you set your heart to accomplish His will, 1 John 5 and other passages assure you He will bring it to pass in His time.

Another encouraging thought is to know that Jesus' main work at this time is that of intercession. The Scriptures clearly spell this out: "who is even at the right hand of God, who also maketh intercession for us" (Rom. 8:34, KJV) and "wherefore he is able also to save them to the uttermost that come unto God by him, seeing he ever liveth to make intercession for them (Heb. 7:25, KJV)." Jesus knows what you need and will pray it for you. What a privilege to join Him in His daily work!

Another tactic Satan will use is "What if . . .," to make you uncertain of the future or to remind you of possible problems. Again, knowing this is God's will and that He will help you reach His goal for you, can give you the confidence to silence such thoughts.

Take courage in the knowledge that the longest journey is accomplished only one step at a time. If you were to walk one hundred miles, you might give up before starting if you looked at how many steps that would take or contemplated the many obstacles or problems that might arise along the way. So trust the Lord and launch into the process. He will take you safely through in His time. Recognize also that it is laid out in steps—simple steps you can take at your own pace for an easier journey.

Other things you can do to make the process easier and better ensure success are:

Establish winning habits.

Cultivate an open heart. Let the Lord teach you what to do. Be open to change, for you have seen from the chart that, unless you are already a powerful house of prayer, you are falling short of Jesus' standard for you as church.

Allocate personal time in the Word and for prayer. Only if these are being strengthened in your own life can you expect to see success. You've needed these all along; your ministry cannot be all God wants it to be if you have allowed these to be squeezed out. A sign recently heard of unfortunately is too close to the truth of what many practice: "If your day is too busy, forget about having your devotions," signed Satan.

If this is true of you, then try a two-week experiment (resource 2) of setting your time with the Lord as your first and highest priority for the day. Try to keep track of how these fourteen days go. Were they as hectic? As many things go wrong? Pressures as great? How were you at the end of each day? As fatigued, worried, overwhelmed? You should definitely find that when you invite the Lord to start your day with you, that He will smooth things out much more than on those days when you leave Him out.

Eliminate distractions. When you aim at something with eternal value, you can be certain the enemy will try to sidetrack you, bring in distractions. Take note of things which tend to swallow up your time and eliminate or minimize them. Ask the Lord to stop or cut down on such distractions and to show you anything you need to do in this process.

Commit your day to the Lord when you first get up. Ask Him to order it, to keep you on His track, and to eliminate any unnecessary interruptions or distractions such as people walking in. If the phone is a problem, ask Him to let only those people He wants you to talk with, call you. You may also consider, if you are not already doing so and it is feasible, having your calls screened so the less important ones can be handled by another or a message concerning the subject is taken. It may even mean using an answering machine for those with little or no staff.

This will eliminate long conversations during those times you need to be focused on your work at hand. Another help is to have certain blocked-out hours where everyone knows you are not available except in an emergency.

Cooperate with your leadership. The enemy will do everything he can to keep you from succeeding. If he knows he cannot stop you from developing prayer, then he will try to bring dissension in the ranks. Also cooperate with leaders from other churches and prayer groups, learning from them, taking from them the things which are transferable to your congregation. Don't let the enemy throw up roadblocks of differing theological stands. This is a smoke screen he uses effectively to keep us from being unified in prayer.

In the human body the hands, the legs, the mouth, the ear can all be different and yet cooperate beautifully in certain functions to make the body work as one. A healthy body does not compete with itself. Each part allows all other parts to function as they were designed. Nor do they criticize the differences between them, but appreciate the contribution each is making so the whole body can work smoothly and successfully. Churches, the Body of Christ, can have differences but cooperate in those areas that will make stronger, healthier churches.

Reject negative thoughts. Your mind is the key to all the enemy's attacks. If he can get you to believe a lie or half truth, then he can defeat or weaken you. Therefore, if you find negative thoughts coming about another person, especially in relation to prayer, simply choose not to accept that thought. Often an effective way to handle such thoughts is to say, "That is not my thought. I choose to believe the best about this person." In this way you are bringing every thought under the control of Jesus as stated in 2 Corinthians 10:5. It may also help to say a positive thing about the person or circumstance being attacked by the enemy. Praise also is another way to stop the enemy's attacks. When dealing with negative people, ask God to let you see them as He sees them.

Finally be committed to the process for the long haul.

Jump Start Needed?

Some of you may feel you are even below the starting level. You see your church declining so fast you could almost call yourselves a perishing church. If you find yourself in a perishing church mode, then do the following emergency action steps to help jump start your church into the first level.

As a pastor and leadership board, you need to individually go before the Lord, seeking His face in confession and humbleness, for Him to show you why your church is in trouble. Take a blank sheet of paper and pledge before the Lord that *whatever* He brings to your mind, no matter how painful, how obscure, you will write it down on the paper. At that point you do not need to deal with it unless He is strongly impressing you with the solution or steps He wants you to take.

Action Step #1

Later you need to look at this in depth. Some of the things you may ask are: What is the role of prayer in our church? Where do we fall short of the mark? What power plays are people doing that cause dissension and division in the church? How can we lovingly address these? Am I part of the problem? What do I need to confess now in order to be a prepared vessel to help lead our church into a significant move of Your Spirit? Am I willing to set aside my desires, goals, ambitions, and prejudices to see our church become all You want it to be? Who do I need to forgive for offending

See resource 5 for materials to help you work through forgiveness.

me—someone in leadership, a lay person, family member, parent, sibling?

Action Step #2   *Gather all the leadership together to implement action steps 1–3.* This is good to do for a weekend retreat where you come before the Lord with no other agenda than to seek His face in heart searching and repentance. Because of your critical need, consider calling in one of the many prayer specialists God has raised up to help lead you through a time of heart searching and cleansing. You may contact our office for the names of those we know who are available to call in.[1] But even before you do that, implement action step 1.

Action Step #3   *Call the church together for a time of heart searching and repentance.* As leadership you need to be willing to say and do the difficult things. Tough love will be the best solution. If one of your leaders is having a significant problem accepting the direction the Spirit is showing you, encourage this person to take it to the Holy Spirit to see if this church is where the Spirit wants him/her to be. If a leader still is not willing to go along, he should consider that maybe he is no longer to be a part of a body that is moving in a direction he is not willing to go. If this becomes the case, then let him go in love; do not condemn him or think less of him for leaving. Accept what he believes to be God's leading for him because you know God is leading you in this direction—this is His will for your church. He will produce the results both you and He desire. It is important to have unity in the church leadership.

Feel a little overwhelmed? A little excited? That is good! The Spirit has most likely been preparing you and your church for a long time. He is ready to lead you through each step to becoming a powerful house of prayer. If you've looked ahead any, you may feel like the little boy on his first day of school looking at the many years of education it will take to become a doctor. He may get panicky. That is what the enemy would like to happen to you as you start this prayer adventure. But remember, don't look at the obstacles. Look at the Lord and each *single* step. Most are easy to take. All should produce measurable results.

As leadership you need to be willing to say and do the difficult things.

▼

Prepare yourselves for an experience you'll never match with any other church activity. The church that comes alive with prayer is a dynamic, powerful church in all areas of ministry. *It will accomplish all God has for it. And the road to reaching God's purposes will be much easier when prayer has gone before, smoothing out many of the otherwise rough places.*

Jesus spoke of the difficulty of putting new wine into old wineskins. It is better to save the old wineskin by releasing it from being exposed to the new, than to see it ripped apart by something to which it cannot yield. At the same time, the new wine must be put into containers so it can accomplish its purposes. Ask the Lord to remake you into new wineskins so you can hold all He has for you.

Remember, the doctor who has a cancer in his own body cannot ignore it any more than he can in his patient. For both, he must take the necessary steps to ensure that all which potentially can kill is removed and the wound cleansed and sutured so it can heal. If he catches the problem early enough, and the Master Physician is his Chief of Surgery in the operation, then the success rate is almost guaranteed. Natural consequences may occur from neglecting the signs of sickness for too long, but one thing is for sure: if the treatment is not given, the patient will die!

Action Steps Summary

1. As a pastor and leadership board, you need to individually go before the Lord, seeking His face in confession and humbleness, for Him to show you why your church is in trouble.

2. Gather all the leadership together to implement action steps 1–3.

3. Call the church together for a time of heart searching and repentance.

Notes

1. Dian Ginter 5575, 24600 Arrowhead Springs Road, San Bernardino, CA 92414.

4

The First Steps
For All Churches

In the time of the Romans, one of the essential elements for a soldier's protection in battle was his shield. It was able to stop many enemy attacks, especially those fiery ones that could appear out of nowhere and do immense damage. For many a soldier, his shield meant the difference between life and death, or at least great wounding. Sometimes important warriors even assigned a man to carry their shield for them for extra protection. Often, when many soldiers would come together to guard the same area, they placed their large shields side by side and formed a hedge-like protection.

The Shield of Prayer

Prayer is the extra protection God allows people to offer when areas of concern in our churches need guarding. Joining together in prayer offers more protection than if church members pray separately. As with the oil illustration, many single drops joined together give much more protection than only a single drop. Greater things can be accomplished when individuals join together.

Ecclesiastes 4:12 tells that a cord of three strands is not easily broken—another apt illustration of this vital truth concerning the need for each other's prayers. In Ephesians 6, the Lord refers to your shield as a shield of faith. Prayer puts your faith shield into position by intercession, asking for His covering to protect each of the leadership and various ministries of your church as well as the congregation. Without such a shield, the enemy can successfully attack with the fiery darts of dissension, disunity, gossip, unkind words, mistrust, pride, lack of self-control, competition, power struggles, fear, or hesitancy. A strong prayer covering can help deflect and neutralize most if not all of what the enemy sends to stop effectiveness for the Lord.

The bigger the target, the more covering it needs. Experience shows that weaker targets also require more protection if they are going to resist the enemy's attacks; therefore, new ministries and weaker individuals need more prayer covering. This is why the Lord says prayer needs to be at the heart of all your church does, and that the church truly must be a house of prayer. Unless this goal is achieved, a church will never reach its full potential and runs the risk of being defeated as the struggles become overwhelming.

Prayer needs to be at the heart of everything.

▼

Too often things which do not have proper prayer covering, no matter how insignificant or how good things may appear, are being done in the flesh because God has not been involved in the endeavor. Churches need to seek God's will initially and then follow it for the activity. This positions God at the center, allowing Him to lead the activity to His desired outcome. Often God will have laid the matter on the heart of several members to pray for His will and/or goals. This usually results in each activity having an effective prayer shield, offering protection so the activity can be the powerful instrument God intends it to be.

The church that successfully follows God's pattern for prayer will be well on its way toward the goal of becoming a powerful house of prayer. It is essential, not optional. Any church can reach such a level if there is a desire and enough knowledge which is put into practice. Since chapter 3 helped you identify where you are in this process, you can now decide how to reach your goal.

Common to all four classifications of churches listed in chapter 3 is the need to have proper groundwork laid which gets maximum results—the greatest impact and participation— in the shortest period of time. The remainder of this chapter gives preliminary steps critical to the success of all churches in their quests to become powerful houses of prayer.

Preparing the Leadership

As you have been reading this book, you should be starting to have some vision of how prayer can impact *your* church. You should be hearing from God some of the plans He has in store for your people. As soon as you become convinced this is where He is leading you, commit the whole process to Him and take the following preliminary action steps.

Cleansing Is Essential

Preliminary Action Step #1: *You and your church leaders must recognize yours, theirs, and the church's shortcomings and need for cleansing.*

There is strong biblical precedent for this first step of confession and repentance. The Lord speaks strongly to several churches in Revelations including telling them if they don't repent He will remove their lampstand (2:4, 5), or will fight them (2:16). Israel had similar standards. Joshua 7 records how Achan's sin was responsible for the whole nation being punished. Later when the whole nation sinned by not letting the land rest, seventy years of captivity resulted, affecting people not yet born (Neh. 1). Only when the people at the end of the seventy years' captivity repented, were they restored to their original state. Reading such passages as Daniel 9:5; Nehemiah 1:6,7; and Jeremiah 8:14 and 14:7 shows these three godly men identifying with the sins of others and confessing them as though they were their own. Such confession seems to clear the way for God to restore and renew that which had been lost because of sin.

It is like a serious, guided diet regimen. One of the things often recommended is to have a one- to three-day cleansing prior to starting the diet. When built-up impurities in the system are eliminated through the cleansing time, a much greater and quicker success is expected in any diet program.

So it is with prayer. It is greatly hampered, often made impossible, because of sin (Ps. 66:18; Isa. 59:2). Thus the spiritual system needs to be cleansed before embarking on any prayer strategy. The importance and impact of this step cannot be over emphasized. Done improperly, you have no chance of becoming a powerful house of prayer.

However, if a few members refuse to go along with the program because of unconfessed sin (rebellion and stubbornness are included in such sins), the very heart desire of the vast majority to pursue this course is sufficient. One of two things probably will happen. Either those resisting this step will let the Lord soften their hearts as His Spirit starts to work in others' lives, or they will become so uncomfortable and dissatisfied in the new, cleansed atmosphere that they will leave. So don't let the few keep the many from following God's leading. Seek Him about how to graciously handle such a situation and people.

This is a step that is important for individuals, groups, and even organizations to do. For example, look at the recent experience of twenty-five of the *top* Christian organizations and denominations that came together to try and work out a unified focus of ministry for a strategic overseas outreach. One of the leader's opening questions was, "What will it take to bring us together in unity?" After a pause, one of the men spoke up and said, "We will need to confess our sins against each other—sins of arrogance, pride, jealousy, and suspicion." Others volunteered many other barriers and sins, enough to fill three blackboards!

Then each of the twenty-five took one sin and confessed it individually for his organization/denomination and for the group as a whole. A precious time of healing and reconciliation flowed from that very crucial start. The resulting unity was unparalleled in any of their previous attempts at working together.

Preliminary Action Step #2: *The leadership (and eventually the congregation) needs to come before the Lord for a confession and heart-searching time, recognizing that they are not the house of prayer He wants them to be.*

As you read the unity illustration above, the Lord may have brought things to mind that need a similar healing. Make note of them. The leadership should admit the things that need to be confessed, so God can help your church reach the house of prayer level. A sample prayer of preparation and invitation follows and provides a pattern of what needs to be said before such a period of confession. Repeat it as is for your own prayer, or put the concepts into your own words.

> Father, You know our church, You know each member of our congregation. We are Yours and desire to be a house of prayer—to be a praying congregation. But to do that, we know we must be clean before You. So please help each one of us to be open and transparent before You. We invite Your Spirit to point out anything that is displeasing to You in our lives or in the life of our congregation. Give us the courage to be willing to say what You want us to say, to submit our will to Yours, and to take whatever steps You show us need to be done. We covenant before You, as leadership today, to be the first ones to let Your Spirit work in our hearts. Enable us to do what You show us. Amen.

Many churches have found that leadership time on a Friday and Saturday retreat provides the atmosphere to deal with intense subjects. An ideal way is through a church prayer summit as offered by Earl Pickard or Ray Bringham. (See resource 4.)

Before such a time of prayer, analyze your church history. In addition to church records, going to older members or those who have moved may help. Be certain to cover such points as church splits and the sins that led to that; wrongly forcing out pastors, staff, or members; any discrimination practiced; or board fights. Also include dissension, power struggles, personality conflicts, or gossip that have been or now are a part of the church life. If you don't know what has gone on, confess anything you think might have happened.

Preliminary Action Step #3: *As you spend time in prayer, list the things God has shown you.* These will be used later by the congregation during their time of confession and heart preparation.

Prayer Coordinator

You need to appoint someone to coordinate this powerful house of prayer project. The sooner you bring the person on board, the better. If you cannot afford the ideal, a full-time minister of prayer, then draw from your staff or congregation. This may be the pastor, if no one else is available, or an appointed leader who has a strong interest in prayer or at least an openness to learn. Another source would be any retired clergy, missionaries, or others who have a burden to pray. You will often find praying laity in mission meetings or the Wednesday night, or equivalent prayer meeting.

Ask the Lord to show you the right person to head this up—a committee might also be a possibility or the leadership board as a whole. No matter who heads it up, the senior pastor must visibly and solidly support the prayer ministry.

Preliminary Action Step #4: *Determine whether you have the finances to hire a full-time, or at least a part-time, minister of prayer or prayer chairman.* Act on this as soon as is expedient. Remember, where your finances are, there your heart is (see Matt. 6:21).

Preliminary Action Step #5: *Ask the Lord to show you someone who can help form a prayer committee or council of Spirit-led, praying people until one is found who would be His person to coordinate prayer.* If you are not able at this time to take on a full-time minister of prayer, or until you can secure one, if you are a large enough church and can afford it and can find the right person, this should be a paid pastoral position, probably with the title "minister of prayer." If not, then this can be done either from the staff or leadership level or from the laity.

Qualifications

Your choice should already have a good prayer life and be willing to learn more and go deeper into this activity. The person needs to have a real heart for prayer, be solidly grounded in the Word, and be one who works well with others. It is always an advantage if the person is one who knows how to lead and whom people like to follow. Above all, the person must have an intimate walk with the Lord and display the fruits of the Spirit (see Gal. 5). Another important prerequisite is humility in his or her walk and not be a "know it all." It is a great help if the person is able to initiate and run the ministry without a lot of supervision. A committee or council could help if necessary for one who is weak in leadership and initiation skills.

This ministry will not prosper or reach its full potential under anyone who does it in his or her own strength, no matter how capable the person may be. Hopefully, although not an absolute requisite, the person should feel comfortable in speaking before people. (Additional good guidelines for the prayer director or coordinator can be found from the materials under "Prayer in the Church" in resource 4.)

If you have no one like this, then ask God to bring someone to your church who does have these qualities, or ask Him to lay a burden of prayer on the heart of one of the members and let Him develop these qualities in the person. Remember, too, people who have such a burden may be in your congregation, but you have yet to discover that part of an individual's life. Ask God to show you any such person. On a piece of paper, write the name of the person whom God has shown you. But if there is no one, then write, "We are praying for someone." Start praying that God will lead His person to have a strong burden for such a ministry, so that when challenged, the individual will already have been praying about being used by Him more in prayer. The person then should see how this opportunity is His answer to his or her prayers.

If you belong to a denomination and feel so led, let it be known to them that you are looking for a prayer coordinator. Many times there are retired clergy who don't want to take on the responsibility of a pulpit but would love to be involved in developing the prayer life of a church.

Preliminary Action Step #6: *Next, write down any ideas you have for starting this project.* As you pray, God will be showing you various things that can be done. Determine who should be involved, when those ideas should be implemented, and do so at the appropriate time.

Preparing the Congregation

When Jim Goforth became the pastor of First Baptist Church in Rusk, Texas, there were four hundred in attendance with an eight hundred membership. It was a very wonderful, old, traditional church which seemed badly in need of spiritual renewal. The pastor initiated a prayer emphasis which included a prayer chain, a prayer room open at all times, prayer teams, and a prayer coordinator. He started incorporating prayer into his sermons, emphasizing its strategic role in all parts of the ministry and lives. Staff members also were encouraged to position prayer at the heart of their life and ministry. He did several other things, including having a conference with a guest speaker to teach a course entitled "Prayer Life." They have seen significant growth, renewal, and impact through prayer on both their congregation and the surrounding community.

Pastor Goforth knows what the key was to unlocking the potential of his church. "For thirty years I preached more prayer than I prayed. But it wasn't until people started seeing praying in my life that my words made a difference. We are fighting on the wrong battlefield. The battle is to be won on our knees. Then we go out and do what God tells us to do. There is no substitute for praying preachers."

No matter where your church is in the process of becoming a house of prayer, the pastor will be the one to lead the process, help impart vision, and set the pace. What he says from the pulpit, along with how he models prayer in his private and public life, will have a significant impact on the effectiveness of your church's prayer strategy. As a pastor (and leadership, too), you immediately start the drawing closer to God steps in resources 1 and 2.

Remember: the teacher only needs to be one lesson ahead of the pupils! Don't let the enemy intimidate or deceive you into thinking you are not qualified enough to lead this movement.

You probably have experienced many times the truth that the pastor often gets more from his sermon than the congregation. So it can be with prayer. You should find the end results are wonderful first in your own life, then for the church as a whole, as well as for each individual who follows through on the process.

See resource 6 for ideas and sample outlines based on the Lord's Prayer.

Also, prepare the congregation through several sermons on the wonderful God you serve and the importance of prayer in getting to know Him. Emphasize how this will make prayer more meaningful as they start to draw closer to Him, getting to know Him on a more intimate level . Be transparent, especially if this is one of your weaker areas. Let them know you will be going through this *together.*

Note: People who have a weak prayer life often feel guilty about it, especially if they are in leadership and definitely if they are the pastor. One of the wonderful things you will gain from this process is a strengthening of your own prayer life, which should help to improve your feelings of self-worth. This will remove one of the "hammers" with which Satan undoubtedly has been hitting you. The next section will address that problem and offer suggestions to solve it.

Involving the Whole Congregation

Having prepared yourself as leadership, you are now ready to bring the congregation into the action. The sermons should have stirred their hearts to consider taking a step of commitment to remove any personal or corporate hindrances of moving toward becoming a powerful house of prayer.

Individual Confession

Preliminary Action Step #1: *Go back to "Preparing the Leadership," action step #2 since probably the whole congregation was not involved in the confession time.* Use this step as a foundation for having everyone come before the Lord in a confession and heart-searching time. You may want to mention some of the things you have written down from your own leadership time of heart searching.

Each individual should be encouraged to take time apart to analyze his or her life, lay it before the Lord and ask Him to show what He wants changed. What still needs to be confessed? What relationships are strained? Is there unforgiveness, even from childhood or while growing up? The role of the Holy Spirit is to reveal just that. Resource 7 has a list of thought questions that can be used in this process.

Preliminary Action Step #2: *Develop materials to help each member draw closer to the Lord by using resources 1, 2, 5, and 7, along with the diagram and discussions on pages 7–10.* These materials could be given in a packet or in Sunday School classes, small groups, or other appropriate settings. You might consider having a special Saturday prayer workshop in which individuals in the congregation can set up their own strategy for drawing closer. You also could use this as a time to include some impartation of vision and foundational training in prayer, as well as a time to pray for the vision, goals, leadership, and each other.

For both leadership and laity, one of the keys to becoming a powerful house of prayer is to get each person to develop a deeper, intimate, personal relationship with God—similar to that with your closest friend or a beloved spouse. (See chapter 1 for a diagram and discussion.) It is from such a relationship that quality prayer flows. Too often prayer is used to get things from God. This kind of pray-er risks being manipulative in prayer times and having a wrong perspective of why he or she prays. Also, opportunities to intercede may be strained and boring if not difficult.

Although the enemy may be a factor in some of this, to a great degree such problems can be from lack of the personal element in your prayer times. The remedy will only come when you really fall in love with God—worshipping Him from the depths of your heart, learning to trust Him completely because of who He is, and drawing so close that you sense the things He wants to see accomplished. In turn your heart responds with prayers flowing out, requesting from Him the very things He wants to see done.

For many, one of the first steps in this process includes growing closer to God as a Father—the protective, caring, understanding parent who wants the very best for His children. But past experiences with less than perfect earthly parents may interfere in such a relationship with God. Steps should be taken to overcome any such hindrances. In resource 5 you will find a section designed to help a person successfully work through such a process.

Congregational Confession

After several messages on prayer, and as you sense the congregation is catching the vision of what prayer can do—they are getting a taste for it and a deepening desire for God to act—you then need to call for a congregational time of confession and heart preparation.

Preliminary Action Step #3: *As leadership, your next step is to spend some time in prayer, asking God what He would have you do in leading the church in a time of confession and heart searching.* In resource 7 there are materials including Scriptures and sample prayers, which can be used in such a time. This will include personal confession and preparation as leadership to enter this undertaking with prepared hearts.

Preliminary Action Step #4: *Take a paper and list out the steps He shows you, along with the areas of specific concerns for confession He brings to mind.* Your list should start with the things He showed you as leadership during your time of confession. Note: something like this will be most effective if those leading the time are transparent themselves.

In confessing any known sin as individuals or as a congregation, be sure to cover such areas as prayerlessness, unforgiveness, cold hearts, lukewarmness, lack of unity or cooperation, power struggles, and backbiting, as well as the normal sins confessed. In the area of spiritual health, the less visible sins are often the ones that hold us back such as gossip, judging, anger, fear, worry, entertaining wrong thoughts, even though we don't act on them, as with lust.

The more open and transparent you are, the greater freedom the Holy Spirit will have to draw you deeper into prayer so that as individuals you will know God more intimately and desire to talk with Him more. Such depth, intimacy, and freedom in talking with God should spill over to your prayers at church so that prayer becomes a natural way of life for your congregation and you truly can become a powerful house of prayer. Resource 8 offers some additional suggestions on how to handle this step. Develop a plan of action from these materials and any other the Lord leads you to take based on your specific make up and needs as a congregation. (Note: Several individuals may find it too difficult to approach God at the greater intimacy level. They will find it more comfortable to make their closeness stay at a dearly loved child/parent relationship. It is less threatening and for many entails fewer barriers to hinder their progress. But they will need to be certain they are not stopping anything the Spirit of God wants to do in their life.)

Once a number within your congregation start developing this new relationship, you should also see a difference in your prayer meetings. Because people will be understanding God's heart more and starting to feel as He feels, the dynamics of prayer should change. No longer will prayer be a seen as a duty or something to dread. It will be seen as a privilege and be anticipated. You should start noting an air of expectancy in people and an increase in answers to prayer.

Dedication Service

The whole congregation is now ready to dedicate itself to becoming a powerful house of prayer.

Preliminary Action Step #5: *Ask the Lord to show you what would be the best congregational format of dedication to becoming a powerful house of prayer.* This may be during your worship service or a specially called service for the whole congregation. You may want to consider including things like a formal signing of a pledge to the Lord, a recited prayer in unison, a time of individual prayers at mikes in the audience, or even a candlelight service. Be as creative as possible. The more meaningful and special the service, the more it may impact those who are a little hesitant. This service may need to be repeated annually or however the Lord leads.

Preliminary Action Step #6: *Encourage people to get together in groups to pray for various church and individual needs.* Two or more men or women might want to meet for prayer once a week over breakfast, over coffee or lunch. Teenagers may meet during lunch or before or after school. There can be a Saturday morning prayer breakfast, a midweek prayer time where people break up into small groups to pray for requests given ahead of time (through the offering plate the previous Sunday, in a box in the entrance way, in the office, etc.). See resource 9 for more ideas and suggestions.

It is good to get people praying together, two by two, in small groups, as well as in larger meetings. But realize that some people may never have prayed out loud or are intimidated to do so.

How intimidating can prayer be? Coauthor Dian Ginter relates the following experience.

There I was, my first meeting with the National Prayer Committee. As Vonette Bright's personal assistant for special prayer projects, I was traveling with her and had been asked to be the secretary/treasurer for the committee which she chaired. I was excited to meet some of the great names in prayer: Evelyn Christenson, Dick Eastman, David Bryant, Glenn Sheppard, Jim and Joy Dawson, Norval Hadley, and, of course, my boss, Vonette. What an honor to be able to serve these people. I was in awe. But when I learned that we all were going to pray before the meeting started, I panicked. I knew I was expected to pray, too.

Despite my background as a speech teacher, with seminary training, on staff of Campus Crusade for thirteen years, and even as a world traveler, I was highly intimidated. I knew there was no way I would not look foolish in their eyes! How could I possibly pray like they would? I didn't have the depth or experience of these pray-ers. How could I gracefully escape this situation until they had finished?

The thought crossed my mind to leave, but there was no real excuse I could dream up to cover my fear. So I stayed and I did pray, but only after a very quick, desperate, silent prayer. I begged the Lord to keep me from sounding immature or freezing up. He graciously intervened and I was able to pray with ease—much to my surprise and relief. I found these people I had put on a prayer pedestal were as down to earth in their praying as anyone. I discovered my fears were unfounded. The close relationship that developed made me thankful I had not bolted from the room as I first felt like doing. Praying with them became a joy and a privilege. The enemy's attempt to intimidate me failed, even though it was a strong attack. Someone who is not as strong willed as I may easily have given in to the temptation to decline to pray.

Many people are intimidated when they pray with those outside their peer group.
▼

This is a problem of which you will need to be aware when trying to form prayer groups. Many people are intimidated when praying with those they feel are above their level or peer group (leadership, business people, etc.). The secretary or housewife may not feel comfortable praying with the CEO of a company, the pastoral staff, or deacons. She may have better prayer skills than they but still feel intimidated. Remember, the enemy will use whatever he can to stop prayer. Try to be sensitive when forming prayer groups. Natural affinity groups, friends, and same age groupings can be helpful in breaking down this wall of resistance. This does not mean that leadership should not meet with groups, but you will need to be aware of this dynamic and the possibility of inhibiting people.

Sometimes praying for one subject at a time (conversational praying in resource 9) can help minimize the threat. Another factor is to encourage people to pray out loud at home, first alone and then with family members, so they get used to hearing their voice in prayer. Often times how people pray at home is the way they will pray in public.

Vision Through Resources

"Where there is no vision, the people perish" (Prov. 29:18, KJV). An important part in prayer is the level of our faith, and vision is a key factor in increasing our faith. The church needs to catch the vision for the importance of prayer and the power God releases through the prayers of His Spirit-filled body. Teaching, observing and modeling are key elements in this step. Look at the following three steps as divisions of vision through resources.

Preliminary Action Step # 7: *The first element in increasing vision is to choose several key books on prayer to recommend to your congregation.*

Resource 4 in this book is an annotated bibliography. Under the "Teaching" and "Biography" sections, select several items and ask God to show you through them how to expand your vision. You may want to start with *Praying Hyde*. Also, items by Andrew Murray are always encouraging and help to stretch vision.

The prayer coordinator, an interested lay person or church librarian should head up this project. Deacons, elders, or staff can each be asked to read one and report back to the group. Share such insights with the congregation. A summary could be put in the church newsletter or as an insert in the bulletin. Three-hole punch such hand-outs and save them. Make notebooks available to the congregation— four dollars to six dollars a piece will usually cover the cost for a bulletin insert size and can be collected from each member receiving one.

Preliminary Action Step #8: *The second vision element is to buy several good books on prayer for your church library or have them available through the church office.*

If appropriate, have a book report put into the church newsletter or bulletin. Choose six or more from the annotated bibliography in resource 4, and write them down along with your thoughts on what steps to take in this area. You probably will want to include who will be responsible for the overall reading project, what budget you might have, and how to get the information out to your people in an attractive, appealing manner. (Tapes and videos are also listed.)

Preliminary Action Step #9: *For your third vision element, show J. Edwin Orr's film on prayer and revival to the congregation at the beginning of your quest to grow in prayer.*

To catch a vision of what God has done through prayer in post-biblical times, one of the most dynamic eye-openers available is Orr's "The Role of Prayer in Spiritual Awakening," a wonderful film on prayer and revival. (Also available in video format; see resource 4 under "Videos.") He covers many exciting moves of God's Spirit through prayer and revival and how society has been impacted by it.

For example, Orr relates how when revival was occurring in Portland, Oregon, earlier this century, 110 stores voluntarily closed down from 11 A.M. to 1 P.M. so their employees could participate in prayer meetings. He also shares how in Wales during revivals in the 1800s the donkeys in the coal mines refused to budge. Why? Because the foul mouthed miners were so changed that the poor donkeys couldn't understand their clean versions of commands. These are but two of many fascinating illustrations from Dr. Orr's film. He goes on to show how society was dramatically changed for the good by revival, with crime radically reduced, churches bulging, liquor stores going broke, and biblical morality once more being the standard for the nation.

Your people should be able to see a great parallel between these happenings and how God wants to do the same for you today. Many people have caught just such a vision as they watched this film for the first time. They have come to realize what God can and will do through them if they are open to Him in prayer used to release His power in all areas of life.

If appropriate, after the film showing ask for audience feedback. Have some prepared questions for interaction on the film (see resource 10).

Preliminary Action Step #10: *Use the survey in resource 11 to help identify important prayer targets for your church.* You need to have a number of targets. Also, you may want to identify which ones to aim at first and which can be accomplished down the line. If appropriate, set a time frame to give yourself guidelines and to evaluate your progress.

As you work through these various steps, change is inevitable. Even if your congregation does not fully achieve all steps outlined in the suggestions, you nevertheless should find your church greatly impacted by the improvement in individuals and those practices that do get adopted within the church. Whatever is able to be accomplished can only make you the winner, for prayer is much like the Word of God: it never comes back to the Lord without accomplishing much for Him.

Preliminary Action Step #11: *Share prayer answers. Knowledge of results is a very encouraging and stimulating to prayer. It also helps increase faith.*

Various ways to share results from the pulpit are in the bulletin as an insert, in the church newsletter, by the one receiving the answer at prayer meetings, and in your small groups. Large churches may even have a prayer hotline with both requests as well as answers and praises available. Make it short but sharp. Testimonies might be coached if appropriate to keep them from taking too long. Put down your ideas and the steps you want to take to give both visual and oral feedback to your congregation. Choose a method that will let the most people hear and be encouraged. We all want to succeed and will work harder when we have positive reinforcement.

A Couple More

Preliminary Action Step #12: *Throughout this process, the pastor should continue to emphasize the need to draw closer to God.* Sermons should periodically reinforce this concept, giving new ideas and fresh approaches. Some of the best materials will undoubtedly be drawn from the pastor's own experience. He also may want to allow those who are successful and finding this encouraging to them, for example, to share either from the platform or in a church newsletter format.

Preliminary Action Step #13: *Have leadership and laity, if possible, praying for the pastor each Sunday before he speaks.* This can often be done in the pastor's study. Resource 12 outlines how to do this.

Optional Steps

The following are optional steps but ones highly recommended.

- *The pastor, and any others so led, should pray in the sanctuary for the congregation during the week or on Sunday morning before anyone comes.* Actually praying over the seats, especially where particular people sit, can provide a powerful way of praying very specifically for that person.

Coauthor Glen Martin can testify to the effectiveness of this step. Early each Sunday morning and often during the week, he will be found praying over the various pews in the church sanctuary.

I've found that, being creatures of habit, people have a tendency to sit in the same seats or general area every Sunday. I am therefore able to pray for many of my people by name as I stand by where they usually sit. It gives me a sense of closeness and deeper commitment to those God has called me to serve. I am convinced I have seen lives changed because of these prayers. To me this commitment to prayer is an important and effective part of my ministry. It is not unusual to see God do the seemingly impossible in answer to prayer.

Martin often will pray for needs, for character qualities for the individual, for general and specific blessings in certain areas of their lives such as marital and family relationships. When members of the congregation realize he is praying for them by name—often at 6 A.M. on Sunday morning—they are deeply touched. This one prayer factor alone has done much to strengthen his relationship with what otherwise might be difficult members of the congregation.

- *A very vital step will be to have two or more members who gather either with or without the pastor or as a pastoral prayer support group* (see resource 12). Their goal will be to provide a more intense level of prayer covering for him. This may be on a weekly basis. They should also be committed to praying daily for him, his wife, and family.

- *Praying for each other and needs of the church over the phone can be powerful.* This is also a good way to ensure consistent prayer in case a member of a prayer team is unable to meet at the regular time or there is a need for prayer between regular meetings.

- *Prayer triplets and huddles* (see explanation resource 9) are easy formats to use in generating a lot of prayer for individual, church, missionary, community, national, and international needs.

Just watch the atmosphere change! Prayer will impact many areas including the spiritual health and vitality of the church body and individuals, finances, evangelism, relationships, and attendance.

After working through these general steps, you are ready to apply the specific steps for your type of congregation: promising, progressing, productive, or powerful.

If you are a powerful church, you may find that several, if not all, of the following are already incorporated into your ministry. Simply add any that are not, and then go onto the material designed specifically for the powerful church.

A word of caution: It will be important for those who are catching the vision, who are increasing their prayer skills, not to fall into Satan's trap of making you feel superior to those who have not advanced as rapidly. It is also important for those who are finding this a more difficult task than others do not to get discouraged or feel they can never reach the goal. Each person progresses at different rates, but God is there, helping everyone reach the goal at his or her own pace. Just don't use that as an excuse not to try to advance at the rate God desires.

Action Steps Summary

Preparing Leadership

1. Evaluate this program.
2. Time of confession and heart searching for leaders.
3. Pray and list things God shows you.
4. Determine if you can have part-time or full-time minister of prayer.
5. Ask God for a prayer coordinator.

Preparing the Congregation

1. Prepare the congregation with several sermons.

Involving the Whole Congregation

1. Time of confession and heart searching for congregation.
2. Develop materials to help members draw closer to the Lord.
3. Ask God's guidance for leading church confession and heart searching.
4. List the steps God shows you.
5. Ask God's decision for best format for church to become a powerful house of prayer.
6. Encourage prayer groups for various church and individual needs.
7. Recommend key books on prayer to your congregation.
8. Buy key books on prayer for church library and office.
9. Show Dr. Orr's film.
10. Use survey in resource 11 to list prayer targets for your church.
11. Share prayer answers.
12. Continue to emphasize the need to draw closer.
13. Ask laity to pray for the pastor each Sunday before he preaches.

5

The Promising Church

Pastor Henry is loved by everyone. He has a nice, easy manner in his messages, yet is never too aggressive in confronting issues that could offend. The church is relatively new, but does not seem to grow much. It reached a certain level and hung around that number for the last several years.

Prayer in the church? Of course. Pastor Henry would find it unthinkable *not* to open and close his sermons with prayer. The same is true for meetings and Sunday School classes. Prayer *is* important, but is never really emphasized and is relegated to the older folks—those dear ladies who have nothing better to do than pray for the church and pastor.

The church had had a formal prayer meeting time, but that really never went over very well. It eventually died a natural death. Several were heard to say under their breath, "Praise the Lord!" when they were told of its cancellation, a few were bored by it yet felt obligated to go if for no other reason than to support the pastor; others went because they felt guilty and not spiritual enough if they didn't attend. So the pile they had been under had suddenly been removed by its demise. Boy, were they relieved! Others were a little saddened, for they thought it reflected badly on the church, but they figured there's no use beating a dead horse.

Those who pray regularly find it frustrating to try to drum up interest in prayer in the church. Several have covenanted to pray for various activities and the church staff, but it really has never gotten much beyond that. Others have asked God to teach them more about prayer, but so far their skills are not well developed. But they are open.

Is this familiar? A version of your church? If so, then you may well be a promising church. (See survey pp. 27–28.)

The promising church has a low level of will and skill.

It has minimal prayer ministry with little exposure to prayer trainings.

▼

Overview

Take a look at the typical promising church. It may be a new or an older one. Its prayer life will be very minimal, in part because of lack of exposure to the steps it takes to have a dynamic prayer ministry in a church. Usually more indifference or frustration in prayer exists than resistance to it. If properly challenged and helped, a promising church can easily become a productive church and be well on its way to become a powerful house of prayer.

The key to change for the promising church will be the desire to change, and the courage and persistence to take the steps to change. The Lord says that if you draw closer to Him, then He will draw closer to you (see Jas. 4:8). This is true for churches as well as individuals. Prayer is such a key part of the drawing closer process. Not only are the confession and self- and church examination important, from chapter 3, but the need to draw closer to the Lord will be pivotal in determining if you will be able to move successfully from a promising church to a powerful church. Unless individuals are changed, the whole can never be changed satisfactorily.

By now you should have in place all of the steps from chapter 3. As a result, you may be very close to being a productive church. But the remainder of this chapter outlines four important steps to take before going on to chapter 7. You may find you already are doing some of these steps.

These steps will help develop a promising church into a productive church.

Vision Through Modeling

Much in life is learned through modeling. The baby imitates his parents, the teenager copies the latest fads, and adults keep up with the Joneses. So, too, in prayer much can be learned from observing others.

Action Step #1   *Create vision by observing another church or group in your area that already has a vital prayer ministry.* If you do not know for certain they are doing something different and worth observing, you may want first to contact someone in charge to ask questions and set up an observation time. Ask one or more of your people to attend their prayer times. Once there hopefully they will see some different styles of prayer modeled. Learn from them and put into practice those things that are appropriate for your people. (You don't have to agree completely with them in theology and practice. See what is transferable to your congregation.)

Encourage your members to attend such times of prayer to see it modeled. If possible and desirable, ask the other church to help you at your facility in modeling some of the transferable prayer styles, doing a seminar for you, or sharing at a meeting or Sunday morning what God is doing in their congregation through prayer.

List the names of those churches you would like to contact. If you are fortunate enough to have more than one group available, you would be wise to observe several. If you do not know of anyone in your area you can visit, then consider sending your prayer coordinator/minister of prayer, preferably, and anyone else to another city to observe what they are doing. If two or more go, you will have better results, for they will reinforce and encourage each other.

Expect the enemy to try to bring discouragement in different forms. Typical will be those who will not want to change or who say, "We tried that before and it didn't work." Remember, just because it didn't work in the past does not mean it won't work now.

Several factors are involved which make *now* different from *before*. You are a different mix in your congregation; times have changed; the Holy Spirit is doing a new work in these end-time days, especially in the area of prayer. The timing may greatly impact the results now compared to before. God wants us to be maturing, so when we truly want what He wants, He will lead us and enable our efforts to accomplish all He is laying on our hearts to do.

Increase vision by recommending that most, if not all, key leadership and other interested laity attend prayer conferences or seminars in your area. If there are Concerts of Prayer, be sure to attend. Send a representative to other areas where prayer training conferences are held. Bring in a person skilled in helping churches start a vital prayer movement. See the bibliography section in resource 4 under "Prayer in the Church" for suggestions. Encourage your people to apply and try out new ideas they get.

Action Step #2

Vitality and Variety

Having increased your vision by visiting and training, you are now ready for the next steps in becoming a productive church. The focus is on increasing your vitality and variety. They are interlinked and help to make prayer more enjoyable. You need to ask God to give you such vitality and to show you the ways to do it for your particular situation. Exposing yourselves to a variety of prayer styles as well as prayer experiences is one way to help do this. As you bring these elements into your prayer times, you should find more interest in prayer and longer times spent, because it is not so boring or threatening. Also, variety helps more people find something that challenges them or fits into their style of praying so they feel more comfortable with it. Variety contributes to vision as people see new ways of praying and get "turned on to prayer."

Action Step #3   *Study resource 9, "Prayers and Praying," and choose one or more you are not using currently that would be appropriate for your congregation.* Make a list of those you chose. Next select one and have the leadership learn it, then practice it alone (where appropriate) and together in meetings. Finally, teach those who are leading small groups and Sunday School classes how to lead in this type of prayer. Such prayer modeling will help members expand their understanding of prayer and see new and meaningful ways they can pray. You will need to be using at least twelve of these before you can consider yourself qualified for the next level. (Other elements also will need to be included before you reach such a level.)

Are you now a productive church? Well, take the thirty-question test in chapter 3 again and see how you have changed. Which questions show you still need some work in those areas? Focus on them. As soon as you reach the desired level, turn to chapter 7 and start working on this new level. Also, look through the steps in chapter 6 to see if there are any ideas there that may help you in your goal.

The real key to evaluating your success will lie in three areas.

- First and foremost will be what happens to the individuals at home in their own prayer times. Are they growing closer to the Lord because of their times in prayer? Leadership must be at the forefront of this process.

- Secondly, a noted increase of vision and viability—letting them see they *can* get out of their rut and prosper in prayer.

- Thirdly, the amount of new emphasis and variety given to prayer in church activities, from the pulpit down through the smallest groups, will be crucial.

Many should be drawing closer to God and seeing their prayers really answered. Excitement about answered prayer, its role and impact in their lives, should be increasing. Ideally prayer should be one of the first things people think to do when they meet. The pulpit, Sunday School classes, and small groups should reflect the heightened importance and influence of prayer.

Are your people becoming "prayer oriented"? Is it becoming more natural and meaningful for individuals to pray for each other, to incorporate prayer into their meetings, to see prayer as playing a key role in making things work, and in helping to solve problems? When you can say yes to these questions, you will have crossed over into the productive church.

Take time as a congregation to thank and praise the Lord for His working in your lives. Perhaps set aside a weekend of praise and worship or at least a Sunday service to do just that.

Action Steps Summary

1. Learn from the prayer ministry of nearby churches.
2. Attend prayer conferences and seminars in your area.
3. Work through resource 9.
4. Thank and praise God for His working in your church.

6

The Progressing Church

Many older "status quo" or declining churches will find themselves in the progressing church classification. They may have a small combination of members from the promising, the productive and even the powerful church mentality, but not enough to alter significantly their classification. There is hope! God wants His body to be healthy and strong. He provides strengthening ways for those that have been weakened. Scripture overflows with encouragement through instruction on how to do that. The progressing church can be turned around *if* the leadership and members wants it. Foundational to this is recognizing the problem and then taking the steps necessary to put prayer in its proper place—at the heart of all that is done.

People who have been traumatized by a crisis often feel cut off from the past and a little afraid of the future. They sense disorientation and feel somewhat lost. When someone is mired in such a crisis, author Julias Segal insists that the smallest action may be the key to survival. He relates a story in his book, *Winning Life's Toughest Battles*, about a traveler convinced that he was going the wrong way on the wrong road.

He stopped his car, rolled down the window, and said to a passerby, "Friend, I need help. I'm lost."

The villager looked at him a moment and said, "Do you know where you are?"

"Yes," said the traveler. "I saw the name of the village when I entered."

The man nodded his head and asked, "Do you know where you want to be?"

"Yes," the traveler replied and named his destination.

The progressing church has low will and a medium amount of skills.
It probably has had vital prayer times in the past, but most members are not praying much now.
▼

The villager looked away for a moment and then said, "You ain't lost. You just need directions."

Frequently when overwhelmed with crises after crises, program after program, event after event, you may feel exhausted and powerless—like you no longer can endure, and the search for God's input to lives and circumstances ends only in silence. Little do you realize that countless little steps can be taken. Your church appears to be making great time, but may be going down the wrong road. "We ain't lost. We just need direction." This is the progressing church.

Overview

The typical progressing church will be one that has been around for some time and may have had some significant prayer meetings in the past. But as time has gone by and routine has set in, prayer has lost its freshness. Prayer meetings have deteriorated to only the "faithful," and even then maybe only a few pray, as the others listen or do not participate very much.

Perhaps the women's missionary group, while still praying for missionaries, does not feel excitement in what they are doing, even though they are committed to it and believe in its importance. It is like the housewife who routinely prepares meals but no longer finds it a challenge, a thing to enjoy. She does it because she knows it is necessary.

The "dropouts" from these prayer times may have, at one time, been very powerful in their praying; but now they tend to pray the same things over and over again, much like the leftovers of a meal. The same food, but in a different, warmed up version. Boredom and lack of fulfillment have caused these people no longer to use effectively what used to be a sharp instrument for the Lord.

Some people as they get older also may want to "let others have their turn" now at church and "retire" from many of their church responsibilities, including prayer. Usually, the less involved people are in the church and its activities the weaker will be their burden to pray or vision of what God might do if they did pray more intently.

Other factors that may have helped "kill" prayer as a significant element in a church's ministry are the failures to pray specifically or aggressively, or to let the people know of the results of previous requests. Misunderstandings, hurt feelings, and arguments also contribute to the quenching of the spirit of prayer. Lack of vision—of something worth spending time in prayer or a failure to see its potential—can also produce a spirit of apathy which will cool down a heart once on fire for the Lord.

The following steps will help the progressing church become a productive church. Once the church reaches that level, it can then take the steps which help a productive church become a powerful house of prayer.

Recognition and Repentance

During the preliminary steps outlined in chapter 4, you had a time of repentance. Now you need to go to a deeper level, allowing the Spirit to clear out hindrances to answered prayer and deepen your commitment to drawing closer to Him. First you need to recognize your need by looking at your current situation and the past history of the church. Then take the step of repentance to correct these weaknesses and strongholds of the enemy which are keeping you from reaching God's highest purposes for your church.

These steps are absolutely necessary to progress. It probably will be a painful, yet healing time. Realize that if you were to add only extra prayer into your current situation, without addressing the underlying causes for your present condition, the results would be minimal at best. It would be like putting a bandage over a sliver instead of removing the sliver first. So "bite the bullet" and take the following steps.

Ask the Lord to give you insights into what have been the dynamics in your church history that will help you in recognizing what needs to be done to correct the problems. You should commit yourselves as leadership to be honest and transparent before the Lord in taking ownership as a congregation for what the Lord shows. You may want to contact "old timers" and former pastors who are retired or moved that may be able to give information and insights on identifying past, existing, or potential problems. Example:

Action Step #1

Noteworthy Events in the Church's History

1977 – Church founded after a split
1978 – Called first pastor
1982 – Moved to bigger facilities
1984 – First pastor forced to leave
1986 – Second pastor called
1988 – Pastor sets new vision for the church
1990 – Split
1991 – Second pastor called to large ministry

On an 81/2 x 14 sheet of paper, turned longways, make five columns and head them: Problem, Consequences, Possible Solutions, Suggested Implementation, and Time Frame. As you identify a problem, put it in the left-hand column. You then need to correct whatever you can to reverse the process. Ask the Lord to show you His solution for it and the best steps

Action Step #2

for implementation including His time table. Put this information in the appropriate columns. Ask yourselves, "What happened?" "Why?" "How did this affect prayer?"

Next, go back in church history from its founding. Write a description of why the church was founded. (Was it a Bible study that grew into a church, a church planted by a parent church, or a split-off from another church?) Especially noteworthy is any negative basis for formation such as splits. Example:

Significant Contributors to Growth and/or Decline

1977 – Founded for doctrinal purity and stand on separation
1978-82 – Forced to move to 7 different facilities
1982 – Finds facility to rent and signs lease for 10 years
1984 – First pastor senses lack of support and asked to leave
1986 – Second pastor called, much younger than the first
1987 – Pastor challenges the church to evangelism
1988 – Vision statement written and accepted by congregation
1989 – Second hour of worship (contemporary) is planned
1990 – Split
1991 – Second pastor called to large ministry

Now, list all pastors (of any type), why they were called, and why they left. Check church attendance records, and make a graph showing the church's size at each year from its founding (example below). (Use number units appropriate to your size: increments of 10s, 50s, or 100s.)

After making a line graph of growth/decline, write at the appropriate period in the center, all known significant events in the church from inception, such as building pro-

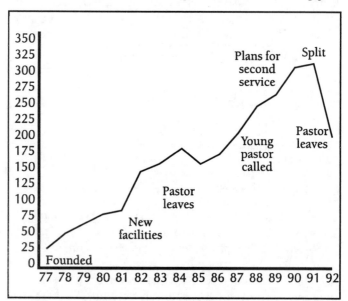

grams, move to new facilities, new pastor, church split, merge with other church—graphing growth, plateau, and decline. Try to identify what contributed to the growth and decline.

Identify, if known, the role of prayer at the inception of the church and during its first five years. Note prayers' strength and contribution to various periods of your church history. The more you can identify, the more insight you may gain as to areas which need prayer. Mark on your chart to the best of your understanding what the role of prayer was in growth periods versus plateaus and declines. Put them in the form of phrases like prayer was strategic, prayer chain, large missionary prayer group, well attended Wednesday night prayer group, intercessors, prayer emphasized in sermons, and meetings bathed in prayer, etc. Note: it may be easier to number your responses and put these numbers on the chart in order to keep it neater.

Action Step #3

Matthew 5:22f incorporates several strong principles on relationships that apply not only to individuals, but to the church as a whole. Sin, whether on an individual or corporate basis, weakens God's fellowship with His children and hinder blessing. In addition, God very clearly says in the Word that the problems created by one generation can be passed on to the subsequent ones (Ex. 34:7; Num. 14:18). Even if the person(s) causing the offense no longer are in the church, you can confess it and ask for forgiveness, since you still represent the instrument by which the person was offended. In Daniel 9:4f the man of God confesses the sins of his people, even though he had probably never participated in them.

Repair and Release

If needed, as a leadership board go to anyone who has been offended or hurt by your church in the past—especially in the area of splits or rejection/removal of staff and ask their forgiveness for the act. Even though the one asking the forgiveness may not have been a member at the time of the wounding, by following this biblical principle, any stronghold the enemy may have had because of the past problems will be removed. Such ignored strongholds often contribute, either directly or indirectly, to on-going problems in a church.

Action Step #4

Church leadership (if not the whole church) needs to release these problems from being "associated" with your church. The following prayer is a sample of what could be prayed to effect such release.

Action Step #5

Dear Father, As a church we acknowledge there have been some real problems in our church history. They are...[list them]. We know these have grieved Your Spirit and ask You to forgive these sins of our predecessors and repair and release our church from the consequences of them.

Re-evaluation

Action Step #6   *In the last ten years and before you obtained this book, what new, fresh, different elements have been introduced into the prayer life of your congregation?* Rate them on a scale of 0 (failure) to 10 (very successful). These could be such things as a prayer seminar, teaching on praise as part of the prayer experience, using prayer in new ways and time in the church life, prayer during church service, people available to pray with others after church service, to name a few. Growth and maturity are important to the health of the individual as well as the group.

Action Step #7   *Identify from this list (or lack of it) several of the strengths and weaknesses in your church prayer life and evaluate why the successful ones work.* How do they contrast to those that are

See resource 13

for suggestions.

▼

not as successful? (People involved? Vision? Timing? Number attending? Crisis in church?) Go before the Lord, asking Him to show you what steps need to be taken to correct any problems. List the problems with the solutions God gives. Where possible, include appropriate verses to claim or guide your thinking.

Action Step #8   *List what things, if any, the church has done to try to adapt to the changes and transitions in society that have also influenced the thinking, responses and emotions of those baby boomers and baby busters.* Take into consideration such things as audios and visuals, shorter attention span, and more simulation and sharper content needed to compete with the media programmed mindset of this TV/video/movie generation. (Churches which have ignored these things have also ignored the changes and impact these phenomena have had on prayer.)

Action Step #9   *List those things you do not use, but that other churches do, to reach baby boomers and baby busters (contemporary service, advertising, videos, concerts, felt need workshops, etc.).* Next to these, list your reasons for not using them.

Action Step #10   *Take the list prayerfully before the Lord, and ask Him if He wants you now to incorporate this element in your church ministry.* Write down what He shows you. After seeking His will, determine your "game plan" and timing to accomplish any changes He shows you.

Make another list of those who know how to pray but no longer do so in an energetic or active way. You may need to ask the person directly for input in identifying what caused the pulling back or loss of interest in praying. What has created reluctance to pray in the way he or she did in the past. Old age? Unanswered prayer? Sin? People they didn't like? Apathy? Boredom? Are they happy this way, or would they like to see prayer once more a dynamic part of their life? If they would, then consider incorporating them into your prayer investigative/decision-making body.

Action Step #11

Have them go through the material in resources 1, 2, and 7. But before doing that, have them take, if appropriate, the following five steps: (1) ask God to show you why you are not praying, (2) repent, (3) ask His help to overcome the problem, (4) start praying and get involved with others, and (5) find someone with whom you can be accountable.

Interview any active pray-er or prayer warrior you have, to see what makes prayer interesting to him or her, and get their suggestions for how to infuse new life into your prayer times. They may also have good insights on why prayer is no longer a vibrant part of your church life. Sometimes you may have prayer warriors that are not very visible. For this reason announce what you want to do and ask that anyone interested contact you.

Action Step #12

Once you have identified those who have a heart for prayer and for the church, challenge them to pray very specifically for the process you are going through in making a powerful house of prayer. Keep them informed of prayer needs. They can become a very strategic prayer covering for you and be instrumental in helping the church turn a corner toward developing a strong prayer base so that it can become all God wants it to be. When advisable, you may want to remind them that a specific prayer concern is confidential. Write those names down.

Using the material in resource 13, adapt and compile a survey to distribute to your membership.

Action Step #13

Compile a summary of responses for each question.

Action Step #14

Develop recommendations and strategies from this list. Brainstorm other ideas. There is a synergistic element in people praying together. Leviticus 26:8 shows that in God's economy five can chase a thousand and one hundred can rout ten thousand. So it is with prayer. Church members deeply committed to prayer should not only pray alone, but in a

Action Step #15

group setting, too. Because modeling is so helpful in prayer, have staff and key leadership join them so they can add to the prayer and more importantly so the members can learn from these seasoned prayer warriors deeper, newer ways to intercede. List all those you want to be involved and set a time for this to occur. All should commit to this as such a vitally important time, only to be missed if an emergency occurs.

Revitalizing Leads to Revival

There is every reason to believe that if you have the fifteen above ingredients in your church prayer times, then you will reverse any decline and be well on the way to having a robust, growing, dynamic, powerful and praying church that will impact your church's sphere of influence for the Lord and place you on the cutting edge of what He wants to accomplish.

Note: Many progressing churches may have a combination of three or four of the types in their church. An older church, especially, may have a congregation with a fairly large percentage being promising Christians who have no real experience or even exposure to a variety of praying style, and have not developed a very healthy prayer life. For them you will want to offer the appropriate steps from the promising church to bring them up to speed with the rest of the congregation. This might be done in a small-group setting or optional evening session or even during a Sunday School time. This would be similar in philosophy to what is offered to new, adult believers to help them get founded in the faith and feel comfortable with more mature believers.

A few members, especially those who have had a consistent walk with the Lord or who have come from praying churches, may be at the productive and even powerful church levels. These will be wonderful resource people, catalysts and models to help implement your above decisions. Be sure to take advantage of Spirit-filled retired people in your church, especially those who have been in ministry.

So now you have come to the point of crossing the threshold into the productive church—your last stop before becoming a powerful house of God. On to chapter 7!

▼

Action Steps Summary

1. Ask God for insights to correct past church problems.
2. Chart the problems on an 81/2 x 14 sheet of paper.
3. Identify role of prayer in church through first five years.
4. Go to hurt members and ask forgiveness.
5. Release problems from being "associated" with your church.
6. Rate fresh, new prayer ideas that have been introduced to your church in the last ten years.
7. From this list identify strengths and weaknesses of your church's prayer life.
8. List how your church has sought to adapt for boomers and busters.
9. List how other churches respond in ways you don't respond.
10. Ask God if He wants any of these elements included in your church.
11. List those who used to pray but no longer do so energetically.
12. Interview any pray-er or prayer warrior for suggestions to infuse new life into church prayer times.
13. Use resource 13 to compile a membership survey.
14. Compile a summary of responses to each question.
15. Develop recommendations and strategies from this.

The Productive Church

There will be effective prayer in several areas of the church, but it will not be developed to the maximum. Notably, significant praying may be going on in the church such as in small groups or at specific weekly prayer times. You may even have one or more prayer warriors along with members who would fall into the powerful church level. But in general, widespread prayer practice is not as high as the desire and openness to learn more about prayer.

The productive church has both a wide range of praying skills and the will to pray, but not a lot of exposure to differing prayer styles.
▼

The exposure to and training in prayer will be important keys in helping the productive church become a powerful house of prayer, and success will in part be based on having and maintaining a strong vision for what prayer can do, along with keeping a focus on advancing in prayer.

Maintaining the status quo for a lengthy period of time can be deadly. This has too frequently been the problem with an older progressing church. It may have once been a productive church, but not had the desire and/or members who were willing to help the church reach its full prayer potential. As with a muscle, flabbiness can set in if the proper "exercise of prayer" is not maintained. To neglect prayer is like neglecting the body. Both bring negative results.

Now that you have gone through the material in the chapter 4, you should find you are well on your way to becoming a powerful church. Vision should be broader, the appreciation of what prayer can accomplish greater, and you should be seeing an anticipation building of experiencing greater depths of God's power through answered prayer. Such expectations should be on both an individual and church ministry level. Watch the atmosphere change. Prayer will impact many areas including the spiritual health and vitality of the church body and individuals, finances, evangelism, your relationships, and attendance.

Evaluate

You will need to take a new inventory of what is going on in your church in the area of prayer now that you have completed the materials in chapter 4. List programs, strengths, and weaknesses.

Action Step #1   *List the following four areas across the top of a separate paper: Ministry, Current Prayer Activities, Evaluation of Each, and Suggestions for Improvement and Additions.* Then put down each area of ministry in your church. This would include the different Sunday School classes, from primary or children on up, and all leadership groups, small groups, boards, fellowships, missionary groups, and associations. List them individually rather than grouping them since often the same interest groups have different formats of operation.

For each area of ministry, write down what prayer activity is occurring and fill in the details under the first three headings. Then think through how it can be improved or enhanced. Different ministries will lend themselves to various approaches. After consulting resource 9, consider such things as more variety; adding a brief teaching on prayer; sentence praying; prayer triplets; more in depth, extended intercession for a meeting and the decisions to be made; having people in another room or at home praying for strategic meetings; during meetings, stopping to pray when a difficult discussion arises; and prayer conferences/retreats.

Action Step #2   *Evaluate your human resources.* Identify and evaluate those people who are pray-ers in your church. Depending on how God leads you, distribute a copy or an adapted copy of the resource 14 survey either to every church member or to each one whom you have identified as being interested in prayer. (You should probably give it to everyone. In this way you may identify some who pray more than you are aware of. It may be a stimulus to those who are not praying to the level they should.) Have them fill it out and return it to you. Then take the completed forms and evaluate them according to the definitions in resource 15. If it is not clear, you can consult with them and have them choose the category they think best fits them.

Action Step #3   *Complete a problem/correction chart like the following one.* List any obstacles you have identified. Include any steps you plan to take to remove them. This can be done by simply praying about it, through implementing a specific plan to correct a deficiency, having a series of sermons on prayer to encourage more enlightened praying (resource 6), or writing articles on prayer for your church newsletter (see resource 19). Often times more than one action is advisable to get the maximum impact for change. Put a check mark in the left box when completed.

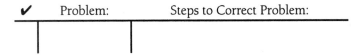

Consider conducting a special class for newcomers in which you introduce various styles of prayer. Also have materials to help them develop their own personal prayer life. The two-week experiment in resource 2 will help them get well established in their quiet times. This will be a true key to having your church become a house of prayer since it starts at home in the individual's heart.

Action Step #4

Make available to all members, copies of appropriate materials in resources 16 and 17. These should be used as a catalyst for people to start praying more specifically for church concerns and for each other.

Action Step #5

List each area of prayer activity in your church in which a person has an opportunity to participate. Such areas may be small group prayer, missionary circle, prayer chain, prayer covering for pastor and staff, prayer partner, prayer triplet, and teacher on prayer. Also list any new areas you would like to develop.

Action Step #6

Placement

List all names of people completing material in action step #2. After seeking the Lord's guidance, indicate under the "Suggested Placement" any new challenges you would like to make to those already involved. This may include such things as are already listed in the above action step #6. It can also involve giving them new responsibilities in prayer such as planning, organizing, teaching, or leading new prayer opportunities.

Action Step #7

You may also, at this time, want to add new names to the list of those who should be challenged but are not yet involved. Help them catch the vision of how God can use their lives to impact His kingdom in a greater way. *Note:* For some it may be wise to show them what is available and then give them an opportunity to choose their own area of interest. In this way they will have more ownership in the decision. This would especially be wise for the more mature pray-er who often needs to hear from God what He wants, rather than from man. Members you challenge should pray about the decision before giving their answer.

List the names of your key people in prayer and the areas of prayer they are involved in on a form like the one below.

Name	Current Participation	Possible Ministry Areas	Suggested Placement	Agreement
1.				
2.				
3.				
4.				
5.				
6.				
7.				
8.				
9.				
10.				

Action Step #8 *For members listed who are under-challenged in the area of prayer, decide on a "Suggested Placement" for them through looking at the ministry "Current Participation" section.* If two or more members who are prayer warriors or spiritual warriors are actively involved, team them up to provide a strong prayer covering for the church and staff—especially the senior pastor. Give them the freedom to choose their own ways to pray for the church, but give them the results of your findings and have them help you in your prayer planning. You will find when people at this level team together for prayer, much more power is released than if they prayed separately. They also encourage each other to greater depths of intercession.

If you have two to four or more members who are intercessors and/or burdened (or prayer and spiritual warriors) and want to pray for the church, use them to pray for the church's ongoing activities and for God to pour out a spirit of intercession on many individuals. See resource 16 for suggestions and sample prayers for this.

Express

Action Step #9 *Ask God to deepen your church family's desire to pray and to help your church become a powerful house of prayer.* This should be a significant amount of time, rather than just a few minutes. It can be combined with a time of confession of anything you identify as still being an obstacle to becoming a powerful house of prayer, especially in the area of attitudes or negligence. Claim the promises in Matthew 21:13 combined with 1 John 5:14–15.

Experiment, Expertise, and Encouragement

As with worship songs, often times you need to experiment with different mixes of prayer styles to see which ones go over the best in your church. Different people respond differently to various approaches. In this ever-changing society, it is wise to be sensitive to the changing needs and tastes in prayer.

Consider the several types of prayer listed in resource 9. Certain foundational types should be included in your mix. You should have at least the following as part of your well-rounded prayer teachings and experiences. Times for:

Action Step #10

- Adoring the Lord
- Confession of sin
- Thanksgiving and appreciation of all the Lord has done and is doing
- Interceding for others
- Asking for yourself
- Praying for the lost
- Conversational praying
- Prayer partners and triplets
- Small groups
- Prayer huddles
- Special interest groups
- Prayer covering
- The difference between defensive and offensive praying
- A study of how God answered prayer in the Scriptures
- A study of God's promises on prayer
- Emergency prayer chain

List prayer areas that are weak and your plan to improve them on the chart below. At the end of three to six months, record your evaluations and recommendations.

Action Step #11

Area of Weakness	Plan to Strengthen	3-6 Month Evaluation & Recommendation	OK

List people you want to utilize in strengthening your prayer focus. They should receive training in how to sharpen and broaden their prayer skills. This can be done by listening to tapes,

Action Step #12

reading good books on prayer (see resource 4), or through conferences, visiting praying churches, and meeting with pray-ers, etc.

Prayer partners or prayer triplets (resource 9) are a very important part of keeping the flame burning in a praying church. As people meet regularly together for prayer, their heart for prayer increases as they seek God for specific things and then see Him answer their requests. You will find an explanation for these in resource 8. There is also a prayer partners covenant in resource 17.

If you are not already involved in the National Day of Prayer, information about the national celebration and contacts in your state can be obtained from National Day of Prayer Task Force, P.O. Box 15616, Colorado Springs, CO 80935-5616; (719) 531-3379.

Action Step #13   *If your church is not too big, consider establishing a Prayer Notebook to record prayer requests and answers for the church in general and its family members.* (Large churches could do this for Sunday School classes and individual small groups.) Include in it all requests that are not of a confidential nature. (See resource 18.) Keep it in a prominent place near your entrance to the sanctuary or at least in the church office. This is also a good tool for the individual.

The person in charge of the book should have good penmanship and be responsible. You may also consider typed or computer generated requests and answers to cut down on the space needed. Try to use at least 10 point type because of the problem many have in reading smaller print. Cards in the pews or sheets in the bulletins or some other way of communicating should be set up. Have a box to receive requests or have them turned in at offering time. Convenience of communication and collection will be a key to making this work.

You may want to consider using this information periodically as a source of praise from the pulpit or in the newsletter. Encourage people to read it regularly. If appropriate, you can incorporate requests and praises in your prayer meeting nights. Staff should also be encouraged to pray for these requests.

Expand and Energize

Your goal is to expand your prayer coverage so that every area of your church will experience God's energizing power through prayer. Therefore, as a productive church you need to be certain your foundational areas are solidly covered with prayer. This means that the following need to have an effective and firm base of prayer:

- Pastor (personal intercessors).
- Staff (lay people committed to praying specifically for them and meeting periodically to pray together).
- Leadership (same as staff).
- Worship service (people praying before and during the service).
- Each ministry (people in and without the ministry praying for its needs).
- Missionaries (people praying regularly for the various requests).

You are growing enough that you need a prayer room to serve as a focal point for many of your prayer activities. Such a room is a wonderful place for people to have a quiet area to pray. It also centralizes the gathering and dispensing of specific prayer requests. There can be a place for a prayer secretary to gather and record information (although we prefer this to be done in another room if space permits), a place for prayer, and another for the phone to pray with people. It is best to have it be a warm, relaxed atmosphere with decorations and maps. You can check in resource 4 under "Churches" to find books and resources showing how to make a prayer room to meet your needs. Terry Teykl's book has drawings showing several styles.

Action Step #14

Add to the list any other area, ministry, or person you choose to cover in prayer. Evaluate the effectiveness of the prayer covering for each, and then take the necessary steps to strengthen any weak areas or to improve those that already are being covered.

Action Step#15

If you have not done so, develop a method of letting people know about good books on prayer. A book review in your church newsletter, or a featured book from your church library are two suggestions. And you will want to have a notebook in your library or church office with all the previous reports.

Action Step #16

Find out about, and inform your membership of prayer conferences in your local area. One good prayer leader, the pastor, or another person in leadership such as the head of your small group ministry, provided you have one, should attend and model different prayer styles to others in leadership as well as the laity. The leader may need to learn the new method and practice it alone with his family or a few others before leading it in public. He will probably want to feel fairly comfortable with the new method before introducing it to a large group.

Action Step #17

Note: We have chosen not to include or comment on praying in tongues because of the mixed feelings and standards different people hold about this subject. Each church should make its own decision on this.

Congratulations! You have now earned the right to call yourself a powerful house of prayer. To double check to see if this is accurate, simply retake the original survey in chapter 3 and see how you now score. If you have all but two or three, then you have crossed over into the powerful house of prayer category. If for any reason you fall short, simply work on the weak areas the survey reveals. Target those areas you feel most important and/or which you can reach the quickest.

Have a time of celebration and thanksgiving to the Lord for the church and a recommitment to your goal of being a powerful house of prayer. You may want to consider where you have come from and where you are now. Statistics could help with that. Make a before-and-after list of what you had when you started reading this book and what you have added—include church growth, the numbers involved in prayer, and finances.

Testimonies would be meaningful, too. Staff and leadership could speak about how they have seen their ministry blessed and made easier through prayer. Lay people should also share how prayer has changed their lives. And don't overlook the children!

You are now ready for the last, yet continuing, step—strengthening yourselves as a powerful house of prayer. Go for it!

▼

Action Steps Summary

1. List every area of ministry in your church under four headings.
2. Evaluate people who are pray-ers in your church and ask them to fill out resource 14.
3. Chart obstacles and steps to remove them.
4. Introduce various styles of prayer to new members.
5. Make materials in resources 16 and 17 available.
6. List each area of prayer where people can participate.
7. List the names of people completing action step 2.
8. Decide where to place in ministry on the list in step 7.
9. Ask God to deepen the church's desire to pray and become a powerful house of prayer.
10. Consider learning to use the various prayer styles in resource 9.
11. Prepare a chart to list weak areas and plans to improve them.
12. List those people you want to utilize in strengthening your prayer focus.
13. Consider a prayer notebook to record prayer requests and answers.
14. Establish a prayer room.
15. Make a list of persons, ministries, or areas to cover in prayer.
16. Develop a method of letting people know about good books on prayer.
17. Inform the membership of prayer conferences in your local area.

The Powerful Church

Significant prayer will be the precursor to virtually any activity, meeting, or undertaking of the church, as well as in the lives of the congregation.

The impact of God's blessing and power on such things as evangelism, church growth, and finances will be evident. Prayer will be very important to both leadership and laity. A wide variety of prayer styles will be used. Probably regular teaching will be available on prayer with either a lay person or staff position heading up the prayer ministry. Prayer conferences and seminars will be attended by many. People will be seen praying for each other spontaneously. If at all possible, a room will be set aside for prayer.

The powerful church is one in which prayer is positioned, theoretically and practically, at the center of all the church does. It is seen as being as important as evangelism, discipleship, and missions.

▼

Covenant to Broaden Ministry

Whether you have always been a powerful house of prayer, or have only recently reached this level, congratulations on the positive atmosphere for prayer. But no matter how much prayer there is, there is still room to become more powerful. Since growth in prayer is essential to church health, consider expanding and deepening the role of prayer in your church by incorporating the following steps. The more your church sees the vision of what God can do through them as a house of prayer, the more effort they will be willing to invest in reaching that goal and the faster you will move toward it.

Having completed those points from chapter 4 that were weak or missing, you now are ready to take some final steps for a powerful church.

Plan a time of recommitment to the goal of being a powerful house of prayer. You may want to have a signed pledge before the Lord, or at least a covenant you all read together.

Action Step #1

Action Step #2   *Families should consider what their pledge will be before the Lord.* This might include individual and family times of prayer or committing to read periodically a book together on prayer. Children as well as adults might enjoy giving a book report to the other family members on one of the great people of prayer like Andrew Murray, *Praying Hyde*, and George Muller. They should separately commit to allowing God to help them become a powerful individual of prayer. Remember, the individuals make up your church family, but individuals live in their own family; the stronger the family is in prayer, the stronger the church family will be.

Action Step #3   *Review chapter 2 and compile a list of steps you still need to accomplish, even though you may have a start on them.* Using the chart below, put down the steps you plan to take to complete them. As each one is completed, put a check mark in the final column. You may have several steps before completing a particular goal, so make your chart flexible, drawing horizontal lines only after you've filled in all the things that need to be done.

Area of Focus	Things Already in Place	Things to Be Done	Finished

Action Step #4   *Keep your prayer momentum up through continued training, modeling, and results reports. Make a chart like the following, listing under each area what current elements you have that support these areas* (small groups, specific Sunday School classes, morning/evening worship services, specific prayer fellowships, etc.). Many an individual and many a church

Area	Continued Training	Modeling	Knowledge of Results

has started out strongly in prayer only to find down the road that prayer has lost its impact and strategic position in their lives. It has again become routine and dull, and not used as often. Power once felt in prayer is no longer there. Don't let the "newness" of prayer wear off. Keep it vibrant and alive. A variety of ideas is offered in resources 2, 4, and 9.

Evaluate if this is sufficient to keep up interest and momentum.

Continue to Draw Closer as Individuals

Already you should be experiencing a closer, more meaningful relationship with the Lord. Review the materials in resource 2 to see if there are some ideas you should add into your time with the Lord—ones that will bring some freshness and variety to your growing relationship with Him. You may also want to review the materials in chapter 1 under "The Wall of Resistance" and "Prayer of Commitment," along with the accompanying note.

The Scriptures say to "delight in the Lord" (Ps. 37:4). This is a step beyond worship and praise. It touches the emotions, the heart, in a deeper way. It only comes as your relationship and your trust deepen. It is like a marriage. You must work on your relationship with God to keep it fresh and meaningful. Seek the Lord with all your heart, and you will find Him (see Ps. 27:4). Psalm 63:1–6 is a beautiful expression of David's desire for God.

O God, you are my God,
earnestly I seek you;
my soul thirsts for you,
my body longs for you,
in a dry and weary land where there is no water.
I have seen you in the sanctuary
and beheld your power and your glory.
Because your love is better than life,
my lips will glorify you.
I will praise you as long as I live,
and in your name I will lift up my hands.
My soul will be satisfied as with the richest of foods;
with singing lips my mouth will praise you.
On my bed I remember you;
I think of you through the watches of the night.

Many believers would like these verses to be true of them, but still have a ways to go before they can truly be able to express such desires toward God.

This is why every Christian needs to ask Him to help them draw near to Him. In fact, James 4:8 says to draw near to God so He will draw near to you.

Action Step #5   *Ask the Lord to help you delight in Him and to see Him more as an Intimate Friend or Lover.*

Your prayer might be something like this:

> Lord, You know I have a problem in expressing my emotions toward You. Sometimes I feel awkward in saying words of deep emotion to You because I have always seen You more like my King than a Lover. Still I know the Scriptures say Jesus is my Husband and I His bride. Yet I relate more to Him as my Savior than as One who has a deep, intimate relationship with me. But I am open and willing to take this step of drawing closer to You. I want to delight in You more; to feel that unreserved joy and acceptance one has with their Beloved; to see You as my all in all; to be flooded with a deep stirring of emotions when I think of how wonderful You truly are; to sense Your unconditional love at all times, no matter how I feel, respond, or what I have done. Help me to pant after You as the psalmist did. Show me anything that is hindering this from happening and how to correct it. Teach me how to do this process. Help me set aside my reservations.

One way you can do this is to start verbalizing words of love to Him. This will help you get used to hearing the words not only thinking them. This is actually a process of developing a deeper faith in the Lord by instructing your heart in the truth of who He really is to you (in contrast to the faulty image you may have developed over the years). Is this not what the Word says? "Faith cometh by hearing, and hearing by the word of God" (Rom. 10:17, KJV). Use as many appropriate Scriptures as possible (such as Ps. 37:4; 42:1; 119:31,32,41,49,92,93) to reinforce these truths. Then allow your emotions to respond to what you are declaring through these truths. The more you do this, the more it will indeed become a part of your belief system.

You may want to write out a list of Scriptures that express confidence and appreciation of God. To start with, go to the Psalms, which are rich with them, as are many of the New Testament books. You may find it helpful to put the verses into categories, such as His nature and attributes (resource 2); His feelings toward you (love, acceptance, complete forgiveness, encouragement, patience, making you into the image of His Son, friendship, etc.); and His help and dependability, or whatever other categories will be meaningful to you as you praise, worship, and thank Him for who He is and what He has done and is doing.

things you tell your spouse. See if these would also be appropriate to tell God. This will help to break down the wall of resistance you may have in expressing your emotions. At first you may feel awkward and rather unnatural doing this, but the more you express these loving words, the more your mind and heart will line up with this as reality. Doing this out loud is also a help. After a time you should start feeling the words you are expressing. Be sure to include some of the thoughts of Scripture, especially if you cannot think of anything to say on your own. To quote Scripture back to the Lord is safe ground and can act as a "prime"; your own feelings and thoughts can flow more easily.

Spiritual Soil

Any successful farmer knows he has several types of soil to work. By cultivating, fertilizing, he will try to bring each type of soil up to its maximum for production. The same is true with your spiritual life. You need to evaluate and then concentrate on allowing the Lord to make your life a rich, fertile ground in which the Spirit can work. Prayer and the Scriptures will be key parts of this process.

Another similar way to look at your relationship, especially in prayer, is to see it as a plant. It needs to be a growing organism that has a life of its own. Like any plant, prayer needs constantly to grow. It will take right soil and proper fertilization, cultivation, sun, water, and pruning to be healthy and produce the maximum effect.

Look at these parallels. The *correct soil* is a heart that is right before God so that your informed, Spirit-led prayer requests can be answered because they echo the heart of the Lord. *Cultivation and fertilization* represent training in prayer and participating with others. The *sun and water* illustrate time spent with God in three ways: reading the Scriptures, being quiet before Him so you can hear from Him, and then talking with God. *Weeding* is done through confessing sin. *Pruning* is eliminating anything between you and God. It may be something good, but by its elimination you can get something better. Often the good becomes the enemy of the best and keeps us from reaching our full potential.

Action Step #6

Write down your responses to the following questions and what you need to do to correct any deficiencies or problems you identify.

- What kind of soil are you (soft and pliable, rocky, hard, dry, resistant)?
- Are you getting enough cultivation and fertilization? If not, what needs to be added?
- What is hindering you from being the best kind of soil?
- Is there any weeding you need to do?

- Any pruning the Lord has been speaking to you about?
- Are you getting enough sun and water?
- Are your "prayer plants" healthy?
- What would make them better?

It is best if you set goals. These will help to hold you more accountable. You may want to share them with someone else, like your spouse or a prayer partner, so they, too, can be praying for you in these areas and lovingly help to hold you accountable. Ask the Lord to help you evaluate where you are in your relationship with Him.

Keep the Vision Visible

Without a vision the people perish. From the pulpit and other places, your vision needs to be expressed periodically. You need to disciple your people in prayer—one on one, in group settings, from the pulpit. Because you undoubtedly will be adding new people to your congregation often, they too will need to be brought up to speed. In their orientation, this vision and goal should be explained and emphasized. They should be shown how they can get involved.

Action Step #7   *The pastor should continue to emphasize prayer in his sermons.* He should integrate it where appropriate into most of the application points of messages. At least once a year, if not a quarter, messages on prayer should be given.

Action Step #8   *If you have not already done so, put a monthly feature article on prayer in your church newsletter.* This could be a teaching section (see examples in resource 19), a biography on men and women of prayer, special answers to prayer in the church family, or testimonies from members who have seen prayer work in their lives. In conjunction with this, develop half sheet handouts on each month's subject that can be used as part of a prayer resource notebook (see resource 16).

Action Step #9   *Give the church family an occasional chance to share their excitement about prayer in a worship service.* Doing this as often as seems appropriate will help people see that everyone can experience significant answers to prayer. The prayer coordinator or pastor would be the logical person to recommend those who have meaningful prayer testimony. If possible, ask that person sharing to practice, writing down what he or she wants to share. In this way you can help the person know what is best to share in the length of time allotted.

Warriors and Foundations

The powerful house of prayer undoubtedly will have or develop those who will be doing real spiritual warfare with the enemy. Those in this category will probably want to have times to "do battle" together. At the same time, when they pray with believers less skilled in warfare, they need to be careful not to go into the strongest warfare in their presence and intimidate or scare them. The well prepared warrior can go out against a Goliath, but to take a foot soldier with him and expose him to the battle may be more than the person can handle. In fact the enemy has been known to use such experiences to cause people to draw back from further involvement in prayer, if not the church.

Be certain your leadership regularly informs spiritual prayer **Action Step #10**
giants and warriors of the crucial things that need prayer covering. Consider such pray-ers to be as key as your pastor. By the time they have reached this level of spiritual maturity, they will be well aware of the necessity to keep confidential whatever they hear. Nevertheless, it is wise to remind them as you initially enlist their prayer support. Be certain to give feedback on their prayers' results.

Offer classes on various aspects of prayer. Classes should be **Action Step #11**
held each quarter either in a Sunday School format, a small group setting or, if you are large enough, as a continuing Christian education course.

Consider bringing prayer into the forefront of your ministry **Action Step #12**
through establishing it as one of two to four foundations for your church. The Church of Joy, a thriving prayer oriented church in Arizona (see chapter 1) uses prayer as one of four pillars for the church: evangelism, prayer, discipleship, and missions. They firmly believe that the centrality of prayer to all they do is a key to their fast growth, dynamic ministries, and financial stability.

An Outside Connection

High on a hill that commands an impressive view of San Bernardino, California, city and the Inland Empire area, at 6 A.M. every Friday, a group of six to ten believers from different churches can be found praying for an hour. From their vantage point they often are praying for specific buildings they see: city hall, various schools, churches, or cults. They have a deep burden for this area. Their prayers are simple but intense, asking God to touch lives, change hearts, and to bring control out of the chaos of gang rule, drive by shootings, drug dealers, occultic practices, and in general the devastating results of sin in their area. Their goal is to see God retake this area through changed hearts and revival. "Your kingdom come, Your will be done in San Bernardino as it is in heaven" is an oft heard prayer.

When the weather turns cold or rain comes, they can be found praying at a local fast food restaurant that welcomes their presence in the back of their establishment. After prayer they enjoy their coffee and conversation for the next hour or so. The power in prayer, the answers seen, the bonding, caring and encouragement that has developed among this group is part of why no one who can misses a Friday. Sometimes they come late, but they come.

The needs of your community, city and state may be great, but your church is not the only one which has a burden for seeing God's will worked in the lives of individuals and government leaders. It is very helpful and encouraging to join with other churches in forming prayer groups that meet weekly to pray for the city. For example, the San Bernardino group is only one of more than six known groups the Lord has raised up to meet throughout the week in that area.

Coauthor Dian Ginter reports:

There is a real move of the Spirit in the Inland Empire with prayer as the driving force He is using to bring about significant changes. The XXXX rated Pussycat Theater, for decades a cancer in the heart of our shopping center, lies in the rubble of its torn down structure, never to be rebuilt as a porno theater. Adult bookstores are faltering and closing down. There is a move to see reconciliation between different ethnic groups. On Friday evenings many can be seen praying together at a different church each week which has opened its doors to this rotating city-wide, cross-denominational, cross-cultural prayer meeting.

The consensus among the prayer groups brings us to the conclusion that the recent changes in the political dynamics of our city council are coming as an answer to prayer. One church has seen a real answer to prayer in regard to young people who have been associated with gang members that have been won to Christ. The church kids have embraced these new converts and have been willing to accept their less than perfect behavior. Salvations and baptisms are on the increase.

Action Step #13 *Sponsor or be part of many opportunities for others in your community to be involved in different types of prayer and developing prayer skills. This should include forming local prayer groups with other churches, participating in or holding Concerts of Prayer, prayer retreats, prayer conferences, or renewal retreats.*

This could be done either at your church or in the church you wish to help. Both would probably be advisable since they should see your groups in action but would also benefit from on-site instruction, modeling and practice. You should help them be aware of the truths set forth in chapter 4 on each person praying within his or her own comfort zone. But also emphasize that they need to "stretch themselves" at the same time to develop significant group prayer.

Consider starting a branch of A.D. 2000, a grassroots, worldwide movement of reaching people for the Lord by the year 2000 in your own community but also focusing on the world, especially the unreached areas. Part of the strategy is to unite believers in a geographic region to pool their efforts in reaching their area for Christ. Prayer is at the heart of all that is being done in this. As a powerful house of prayer, you should be involved in the cutting edge work of the Spirit.

    Prayerfully ask the Lord what He would have you do in this dynamic, evangelistic movement. Your involvement can be a key to helping capture your community for the Lord as you join other believers in seeking His plan for cooperating and strategizing to reach others. As a powerful church of prayer, He may have you spearhead the movement in your locality! This will also help to broaden your vision for the world. Periodically there are vision/on-site prayer trips arranged to various unreached areas of the world. Your prayer warriors may well want to be involved with such on-site praying.

    If you are not aware of any A.D. 2000 branch in your area, contact the organizers at A.D. 2000 and Beyond Movement, 850 Wycliffe Drive, Colorado Springs, CO 80906, (719) 576-7134. Some denominations have plans for similar evangelization. Contact your denominational headquarters.

Also learn about New Life 2000, a parallel movement that is focused even more internationally and is headed by Campus Crusade for Christ. This movement is aimed at reaching the lost worldwide through the Jesus Film wedded with Crusade strategy. Consider a partnership with another city or country in helping to establish churches and outreach centers throughout the world. Dollar for dollar in the nineties, this is one of the best investments for evangelism and discipleship an individual or church can make. There is also the opportunity for your members to go on-site to help evangelize and disciple people in all areas of the world, including the newly opened former Communist nations. For information on this opportunity, contact Roger Brill, 100 Sunport Lane, Orlando, FL 32809-7875; (407) 826-2450. Your denominational headquarters for foreign missions may also help you.

Optional Step #1

Optional Step #2

Power House

On his way to church every Sunday, Baptist pastor Mark Lambert prays for the pastor of a charismatic church as he passes it. What is he praying? That they will collapse or the members will "see the light" and come to his church? No, Pastor Lambert is praying for the pastor to have a powerful sermon, that there will be a strong move of the Spirit drawing hearts to Him, and that the church will have a great impact on San Bernardino and harvest for the kingdom of God. As far as he knows, the other pastor is ignorant of his prayers. It is not as though they are best friends. They are not. Yet Lambert has found this to be a wonderful blessing and encouragement to his walk with the Lord. It has strengthened his commitment to the body and made him more sensitive to the needs of his fellow believers outside his own denomination.

Once you get the "prayer bug," you find yourself on the cutting edge of many things. Look at another area in which this pastor is involved.

Pastor Lambert is Caucasian. He, along with some of his leadership, pray weekly with a wonderful black church. They pray for the welfare of each church; for God to pour out His blessing on them, and for their problems to be solved. The relationship that has developed between the black pastor and his congregation and with Lambert and his people is one of mutual deep respect and love in the Lord. Significant answers to prayer have resulted. Prayer has been instrumental in causing age-old barriers to melt away as these two distinct groups are drawing closer together. They are acting and feeling more like one body. As never before they now cooperate in outreach to the community with no one feeling threatened by the other. They are well on their way to fulfilling Jesus' desire in John 17 for unity.

Prayer has helped to deepen Pastor Lambert's concern and compassion for people as exemplified in the following event.

Racial tensions sparked by a jury trial acquittal caused mass rioting, looting, and burning of Los Angeles neighborhoods in the summer of 1992. Fear gripped hearts. The city of San Bernardino was only a little over an hour's drive from the scenes of destruction. People correctly feared a spillover to their racially tense area. Shootings and lootings soon broke out. In the midst of this, a strange scene occurred in the vicinity of an American Baptist Hispanic church located in one of the most dangerous areas of San Bernardino's inner city. Despite the danger to a white person, Pastor Lambert and one of his elders teamed up with Pastor Navarato, Lambert's counterpart in the Hispanic community. They went door to door to pray for people terrified by the recent events and the real possibility that the burning of Los Angeles would be replicated in their own neighborhood.

People could not believe their eyes or ears as they cautiously answered their doors when these men knocked. They heard Pastor Navarato say in their own language, "We are from the Premier Baptisto Igelisia up the street. We want to know if you have anything for which you would like us to pray. We know things are tense and felt you might like to have someone pray with you." The overwhelming responses were so positive. Suspicious eyes filled with surprise and then welcome expressions as person after person had the strangers pray for them. Many of those people expressed their appreciation and later attended the Hispanic church.

About a year later, more racially tense trials took place in Los Angeles, and again the threat of riots was high. With some foreknowledge of the explosive nature possible from the verdict, pastors spearheaded a concerted effort of targeting the most volatile areas with prayer. Prayer walks through the neighborhoods were organized with local authorities' help, and the potential explosive areas were saturated with intensive prayer. This prayer strategy and the racial cooperation it had brought as they worked and prayed together, were undoubtedly strong factors in keeping a lid on the tension, enough that it never blew up.

Send leaders and pray-ers on-site to pray for others who are not an immediate part of their body. Christians are a body. The body members should help each other. There are several scenarios that can be followed or make up your own.

Optional Step #3

- Go on site to another church to pray alone or with another leader from your church.

- Pray with the pastor/leadership of the other church for their church (and yours, if the other pastor so desires).

- Have praying members of your church go to the other church's worship service to sit in the back and pray for them.

- Invite the pastor, leadership, or other representatives to come to your church so you can pray for them.

If you choose to implement this option, watch the blessing flow, the joy that comes from unselfish praying, and the rewards of bridging any gaps between your church and others. This step can truly have a strong impact among churches and bring a sense of the one body so desperately needed these days. The fruit that results will be lasting, good fruit. As the community sees the real love and concern you have for each other, many residents will move toward the Savior and His people.

Action Step #14   *Consider letting it be known in the community that your church is available to pray for the local people's needs.* People are hurting in your community, but in this fast paced day and age, no one seems to have time to care. Everyone tends to be too centered on himself or herself. Therefore, if you as a local body of believers can reach out to your neighborhood, without expecting anything in return, you can minister to people and often reach some who would otherwise not consider coming to your church.

One way to do this is to go door to door, as you would in evangelism, and say that you are from _____ church and want to know if there is anything you can pray about for them. You may find many who would close the door in your face if you were simply witnessing but who want prayer. This may lead to the opening of other doors in the future. When you do this, be sure and go back and see how God is answering your prayer. Some people go back the first time in two weeks and then about once a month. The Spirit will show you His time table if you choose to implement this strategy.

This strategy can also be applied on an individual basis as the members offer to pray for neighbors, work mates, associates, clients, and customers. Ask the Lord to open up opportunities to pray with hurting, needy people in your sphere of influence. Share with the congregation how God is using you and any transferable ideas He gives you to make your outreach more effective.

Confronting the Enemy

The topic of spiritual warfare in your action steps has been mentioned only briefly because it is so sensitive and extensive. However, some of the principles should be noted here for doing battle with the enemy.

Boldness in prayer will lead you to have boldness in going against what the enemy desires to do in lives. This will come naturally to you both as a church and a congregation. However, do not take any authority over the enemy the Lord does not give you. Be certain you seek the Lord's face. Then do what He says with authority and courage, yet in humility recognizing that it is God who is defeating the enemy through you.

Recognize also that although the enemy is defeated, his roar is loud. He will try to intimidate you, hassle you, and come against you in any way he can. But the Lord clearly says He is greater than our foe, He has defeated him and you need not fear anything or anyone when you are walking in God's protection (Heb. 13:6; 2 Tim. 1:7; 1 John 4:4). The key: to stay under the protection of the Lord and not go out to do battle with the enemy apart from your Commander's leadership. You must not be the initiator; the Holy Spirit must do that in and through you. Daily putting on your spiritual armor (resource 3a) will go a long way in helping you through whatever spiritual warfare you come up against. Then be certain to keep closed all holes in your armor (resource 3b).

Consecration to the Lord

You've come to the end of the Action Steps, even though there are many more you could take. This is only the beginning, for there is always more to learn, always more to discover in God's riches and blessings through prayer.

Hold a consecration service to the Lord as your final, yet on going step. Thank Him for where He has brought you, and covenant before Him to be a consecrated house of prayer. Ask Him to make your church available to Him as a powerful instrument to accomplish His will, to bring His kingdom into the spheres of influences of your church and individual lives. A candlelight ceremony may be appropriate for this, and maybe, once again, plan a renewal of your dedication to being a powerful house of prayer, and having a powerful life of prayer as individuals.

Optional Step #4

Closing Thoughts

Powerful prayer will impact all areas of your church. You should see significant results throughout every part: interpersonal relationships, vision, finances, programs, and evangelism.

One of your goals as a powerful house of prayer will be to reduce the disunity in your body. You should find as people are hearing from God, and really sensing His heart, the strife, division, self-centeredness, gossip, and other divisive tools the enemy uses to damage churches will be lessened. The more the love and caring heart of God flows through people who are praying, the less they will want to do anything that would spoil their relationship with others or with God. Those who are really into praying will become more sensitive to the Spirit's pointing out the less obvious sins which might inhibit their fellowship with the Lord.

As time goes by, you will look back to see you have uncovered only the tip of the prayer iceberg. Your journey to becoming a powerful house of prayer is shorter, but not ended. Just as when you reach adulthood, you find you have not learned everything there is, so it is with prayer. You will always be learning, growing closer to the Lord, and seeing better ways to reach higher levels of prayer skills both individually and as a congregation. You will never want to stop learning or growing, never be satisfied with where you are. The health of your individual and corporate Christian life will depend in a great part upon the health of your prayer life. As in the physical world, to stop growing in your prayer life is to begin declining and start on a slippery slope of deterioration. It may be imperceptible at first, so keep a watchful eye on your growth. Monitor it as you would your own precious health, for your spiritual life is an integral part of your spiritual health.

There is so much more to learn, but with the momentum you have, with hearts that are pure before the Lord, desiring to know and serve Him better, you should find that on both an individual and corporate basis you are and will remain a powerful house of prayer. The excitement of seeing God answer prayers, change lives, move mountains, and do the impossible, and to know that you have had an active part in all of this, will be a great incentive for all to press ever forward in the realm of prayer. May you be like Enoch who walked and talked with God until he reached heaven.

The Watchmen on Your Wall

As you step out in faith to do battle with the enemy in prayer, to take back ground he has held for a long time, you will find attacks coming that need to be intercepted. You will want to gather your prayer warriors to do regular, preventative praying over the church as a whole and individuals and leadership in particular. They can help stop much of the attack the enemy will try to muster to cause you to forsake your prayer journey.

As part of this process, you will want to help your congregation keep before them the vision and goal of strengthening and deepening their prayer life. Chapter 9 provides a tool developed for just that. It will help each individual identify at what prayer life level he or she is and be challenged to go on to the next level.

▼

Action Steps Summary

1. Recommit to the goal of being a powerful house of prayer.
2. Families consider their pledge before the Lord.
3. Review the steps in chapter 2.
4. Make a chart of areas of ministry and list the prayer support for each area.
5. Ask the Lord to help you delight in Him and to see Him more as an intimate Friend.
6. Write responses to questions; write needed corrections.
7. The pastor should continue to emphasize prayer in his sermons.
8. Feature prayer monthly in your newsletter.
9. Give members opportunities to share excitement about prayer in the worship service.
10. Keep prayer warriors informed where crucial prayer needs exist.
11. Offer classes on various aspects of prayer.
12. Establish prayer as one of the foundations for your church.
13. Sponsor and be part of many opportunities to involve the community in different types of prayer opportunities and skills development.
14. Let the community know you will pray for the needs of local people.

(See also five optional steps.)

9

Where Is Your Level?

Babies are adorable. It is fun to watch them "coo" and discover the world around them. They are innocent and vulnerable, needing so much attention. During that time, parents know they will have to change diapers, clean up messes, and in general adjust to care for the little ones.

But how sad it would be if babies did not mature. What if they stayed a children physically and emotionally? How tragic if at the physical age of eight they still had to wear diapers, or if at twelve they had the emotions of a two-year-old. Remember those terrible twos! How would you like to have that kind of trouble all your life from your children? Obviously, no one would. Maturing is the natural, normal, and expected thing—physically, mentally, and emotionally. School tests, doctor's check ups, and the lines on the bedroom wall all help chart a child's physical growth. Right?

But often forgotten is that maturity is both normal and an essential thing to happen spiritually for a healthy Christian walk. There are few measuring sticks for spiritual growth and fewer still for prayer life, but this chapter can help you measure how "tall" you are in your prayer life. Understanding yourself and striving to improve are things God expects of each believer, so determine where your level of praying is, and how to advance to the next level.

"Level of praying?" You may be saying "I've never heard of that before!" It is little wonder if it is a new concept to you. This is a term the authors developed a few years back to increase vision and desire for a greater level of praying. It is gaining popularity as praying people are being exposed to it and see the value of knowing where they are and how they can advance.

Many levels of praying can develop from "now I lay me down to sleep" through the most advanced of spiritual warfare, but look at only the following six levels identified in the membership of a healthy, growing church of the nineties.

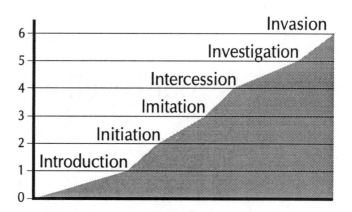

Each church is made up of individuals, so for it to become a powerful house of prayer, its individual members need to grow in their prayer skills. Just as chapter 3 helped you identify the place your church is in its prayer practices, it is helpful for you to identify your level of prayer and be challenged to go on to the next level.

Start by looking at the first level right after the point where you have left the infancy of praying rote prayers such as "God bless Mommy and Daddy and all the missionaries." Each level builds on the next. It is similar to what happens as you learn math. Addition and subtraction form the foundation for multiplication and division, then fractions, square root, and so on. As you advance to each higher level of mathematics, one builds upon the other.

So it is with prayer. The newer levels may be more advanced and complex in their application of the older truths, but they still rely on the foundations of the preceding levels. Also there will be some overlapping between levels, often trying out at first one or more elements of a higher level and then backing off from it for just a while.

Level #1: Introduction

This level is where a believer first starts to realize that it is possible to personally talk to God about those things of concern. Most of the focus is on one's own immediate sphere of interest. Phrases like "Help me..." or "Give me..." are plentiful. It is usually more defensive in its style—asking for protection, for solutions to problems, or for help. At this level you will find yourself praying "I centered prayers" instead of "us" or "we." It usually focuses on yourself.

Many people at this level pray because they have a need to be met or know they should pray, rather than because they really want to. For many, prayer is a burden. Their faith may be growing at this level, but it is probably rather fragile.

If you are at this level, you need to know that the keys to moving on to the next level are practice and burden. First, ask the Lord to teach you more about Himself and prayer. Ask Him to make it more alive and meaningful to you. Then set aside a specific time each day to pray, preferably at the beginning of the day. Use the materials in resource 2, or start out with "7 Minutes with God" a small tract which really helps to lay a foundation for the higher levels. Let this time increase as you learn more about prayer and have a greater desire to pray. Then ask God to help you have a greater burden for what He wants to see accomplished.

Level #2: Initiation

As you develop in prayer, you will start to see growth. This will come as you begin to reach out beyond yourself and your family and broaden your self-centered praying to include a wider scope of requests. Missionaries, crime, drugs, and other concerns will become part of your prayer focus. You will start claiming appropriate Scriptures for a situation.

That includes using the Scriptures to enhance your understanding and vision of what is on God's heart and to start praying back to the Lord the concepts you find in the Word.

For example, Romans 8:28 says that "all things work together for good to them that love God, to them who are the called according to his purpose," (KJV). Know and love that verse, and hold onto it especially when trouble strikes. So when you have a problem, pray something like:

> Father, how reassuring it is to know that You have promised to work everything out together for good in my life. I don't see how this current problem is going to turn out for good, but I know You do and You're in control. So I trust You. Help me wait patiently for You to accomplish what You want to do. Show me how to look at You and not at this problem.

This is the whole emphasis of the Initiation stage. You learn what God is doing and you begin your growth.

Level #3: Imitation

As you move on to the third level, you will become more aware of how others are praying. You may not feel comfortable praying out loud, but you should be sensing a greater desire to learn about prayer. At this level the beginning elements of modeling come specifically into play. This level is caught more than taught—thus the name "Imitation." Whether you are at this level or not, definitely attend seminars on prayer and acquire access to prayer tapes.

Probably you will start reading books on prayer and listening to people teaching about prayer. Books by Andrew Murray, Wesley Duewell, Dick Eastman, Evelyn Christianson, Rosalind Rinker, Larry Lea, and Jack Hayford are just a few of the better ones of a wide variety which are available. (See resource 4.)

As with any new materials, you will want to choose from these authors those things which are appropriate for you and your style of worship. However, don't be afraid to try something new if theologically you have no problems with it. Try lifting your hands in praise to see if this will enhance your worship or experiment with different kinds of prayer. For example, for a few minutes, try only to praise God for who He is and what He does.

Or you may want to incorporate singing and music in your quiet time. Pray the Scriptures back to the Lord. Use a different posture in prayer, such as sitting down, kneeling, being flat on the floor in worship. Broaden the places you spend time in prayer to include such places as in your bath, on a walk, or when driving or doing housework. There is a variety of avenues. Another form of praying that is gaining much popularity in the nineties is that of writing your prayers in a journaling form. (See resource 2 and resource 4; "Drawing Closer to God"; and resource 19, sample #3.)

As part of imitation, many people today are listening on television to teachers such as Larry Lea, who focuses, among other things, on learning how to pray the Lord's Prayer. He and several other authors have devoted books to different styles and elements of prayer. As you listen to them or read their material, many new ideas will be sparked for you which you will want to try out for yourself.

Coauthor Glen Martin has found what so many other believers can testify to.

> For me, one of the best parts of pursuing this level is my deepening relationship with the Lord. Our friendship, my love, my broadening understanding and appreciation of Him, the joy I find in our times together—this and so much more are ample rewards in themselves for working on our relationship in prayer. And the wonderful thing is that it will grow deeper and sweeter from level to level.

I often compare it with my feelings now toward and understanding of my wife, Nancy, in contrast to when we were first married. You know, I thought it was good then. I hadn't any concept of how much better it would get! Yet our relationship took time to develop. Even after all these years of marriage it still does. We try to take one or two hour walks together as often as possible. Why? To talk. These are special times for both of us, and something we both treasure. I'm sure God feels the same about our times with Him.

At some point you'll become very comfortable in this level and will have absorbed these new teachings. You will find your prayer horizons have broadened and your relationship with the Lord has deepened.

Level #4: Intercession

The careful observer would think that intercession has already been a part of the previous levels. So why this particular name? The answer is that at this point, if not somewhat earlier, you should be finding yourself with more of a burden to intercede—a burden which seems to drive you to prayer, causes you to want to spend more time in the Father's presence and bring the needs of others to Him. Thus intercession will become an important focus and consume a large part of your prayer time. Remember, intercession is prayer offered on behalf of others.

Pray for the Lord to show you His heart, His perspective on the things for which you are praying, and to give you His burdens. Ask the Holy Spirit to give you the words to say. You will find prayer becoming easier and easier, as well as knowing what to say, but taking more time because of the many needs you will see and the burden of your heart to have the Lord touch those specific situations and lives. What is happening is that you are feeling what your intimate Friend feels about these situations and prayer is a natural overflow.

See how far you have gotten in just three levels—from at first mainly focusing on yourself to being much more concerned about the welfare of others and of social concerns. No longer are you using only defensive praying. Now you are on the offense, beginning to try to take back ground from the enemy.

Another thing you will notice by this level is that prayer is no longer felt to be an obligation or dull. It is a desirable thing to do. In fact, you may be looking for more time to set aside to pray. This is when you use creative ways like while you are driving, doing housework, standing in lines, or jogging.

At this level you may truly become excited as you really see God at work. Certainly you will be more aware of the power of prayer. Your faith will also be growing as you see these answers, although it may be more dependent upon seeing these answers then it will at the fifth level. In addition, many prayer warriors, new to the arena of intercession, often become overwhelmed by the enormity of the problems they see. It is their tendency to be strong at times and falter when visible results don't come quickly. In part it is because of this flux that there are varying levels of intercession. For a person to grow in his or her prayer skills, the fifth level must become the goal. They must desire to grow.

Have you found your "level"? Look at the remaining two and maybe you can identify yourself or several of the people in your church in one of these levels left.

Level #5: Investigation

You will find your faith increasing to believe God can and will do what is asked for in prayer. There is a reaching out to believe for bigger and greater things. Added to the foundation already laid is the need to learn even more from others about different aspects of prayer. Again, investigating books and listening to tapes, television, videos, and radio will be important. If you have a chance to attend or see a taped presentation by recognized prayer teachers, take the opportunity. Teachers include Dick Eastman, president of Every Home for Christ; Evelyn Christianson, a well-known speaker and author of many books including *What Happens When Women Pray*; Larry Lea, Oklahoma; Fuller Seminary professors C. Peter Wagner and Carl George; John Maxwell, senior pastor of Skyline Wesleyan Church of California; and David Bryant, Concerts of Prayer. Another person recommended is Glenn Sheppard of International Intercessors.

Many people at this level or earlier like to have a partner with whom to pray. Intercession can be even more rewarding when done with others. The prayer dynamic changes some. People often find their partner will trigger a new or at least different depth of insight and prayer response from them. Their partner's approach may be a little different. All in all, praying with a partner often makes one feel they have prayed more deeply and thoroughly about the matter at hand. It can also provide a good check for times when you feel like praying a very strong prayer and would like confirmation this is from the Lord. So, believers who have reached this level of praying and have no partner should try to find a mature, praying believer. Ask the Lord to show you His partner for you.

Now before you look at the sixth and last level, know that *many, if not most good Christians, stop here unless they are actively desiring to reach a higher level of prayer.* Once again, as seen in the Imitation level, modeling becomes a key to unlock this level.

Level #6: Invasion

More and more in the nineties, churches are seeing a number of their members step out in faith onto the level called *Invasion.* Here the term "spiritual warfare" is often heard.

When you operate at this level, your faith and vision will really be at work, definitely growing. Not only are you willing to defend yourself and your loved ones against the attacks of the enemy, but now you "go against the gates of hell." By now you should have a definite sense of the grieving of the Spirit over things and issues. This should always increase your burden to pray. Your joy in praying and seeing God work should also be increasing noticeably. As in previous levels, you will experience an ever deepening, closer, stronger relationship with the Lord. You will have more of a sense of His power and His authority flowing through you as you pray. This naturally increases your depth of faith in Him.

As you try to understand this highest level of prayer, never forget that Satan fears prayer more than any other ministry. A hymn writer put it well when he said, "Satan trembles when he sees one Christian on his knees." If you choose to advance to this level, you will find yourself spending more and more time doing in-depth praying. Your relationship with the Lord, your sensitivity to His prayer goals, and much more will grow. What is incredible is that your hatred of sin and desire to see Satan defeated in all points will increase! It may become an overwhelming passion.

But one final note on spiritual warfare. The 1991 war in the Gulf offers keen insights into the strategies being seen in the arena of spiritual warfare in the nineties. Prayer is like the air assault that preceded the ground war. Wave after wave of air strikes bombarded and knocked out the strongholds of the enemy both in communication and physical elements. Different types of aircraft were used in the assault, depending on the target and nature of its defenses. Without these softening-up attacks, greater losses in the ground war would have been inevitable. Many believers are convinced that prayer was a significant factor in the low casualty rate and quick victory. God gave military leaders wisdom and the strategy which then provided protection for our military men.

Although there are higher levels of prayer in the spiritual warfare arena, for purposes here, these six are sufficient for the growing nineties church: introduction, initiation, imitation, intercession, investigation, and invasion.

Now do you know at which level you are? Do you want to try for the next one? Be encouraged to go on to the remaining levels, to reach your fullest potential in prayer, and to obtain that sweet, meaningful, relationship with the Lord. God is waiting for you. He desires to develop you to the fullest and to use you in a strategic way through prayer to at least the fifth level.

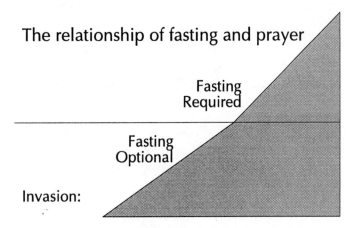

The relationship of fasting and prayer

Fasting
Required

Fasting
Optional

Invasion:

For those who have reached the Invasion level, one other factor can have an impact on prayer—fasting. Whole books have been written on the subject, and you can go more in depth by reading one or more listed under "Fasting" in resource 4. Fasting is desirable and valuable but optional up to a point.

For our purposes, the relationship of fasting and intense praying or spiritual warfare will be covered briefly. Esther and her people (Esth. 4:16) and later Daniel (Dan. 6:18; 9:3), as well as David, Ezra, Nehemiah, and Joel to name a few, used fasts in times of crisis to seek the Lord and His will and favor. Jesus in Matthew 17:21 said that certain levels of spiritual activities required fasting to accomplish a task. Certainly He set the example by both example and in His teachings (Matt. 4:2; 6:16–17; 9:15). The Book of Acts shows fasting as an integral part preceding some important events in the church (Acts 10:30; 14:23).

A fast shows a humbleness and obedience of heart toward the Lord (Ps. 35:13; 69:10) and a desire to sacrifice to be with Him and obey Him. Today people often fast for a specific reason, but others will do it as a way of life to keep themselves in spiritual preparation for intense prayer warfare. Unfortunately, some misuse fasting, feeling that it obligates God to answer their prayers, which is not true or the right perspective and usage.

However, when done with the right motives, fasting is a way of expressing your heart's desire to seek God intently for a specific request or area of focus. It is saying that nothing, not even the basic need for food, is as important as spending time with God or seeking His mind on the matter. Many experience a greater "fine tuning" of their spiritual ears, a clarifying of their thought processes, and a clearing out of the clutter of the world.

Experience and the Word clearly show that fasting is required at certain levels of prayer, where there is a need to break the enemy's longtime stranglehold on a person or a situation. So start fasting early in your prayer life. You should find the results worth the effort.

Consider the following observation and comparison. Just as you want the best for your child, even though you are an imperfect parent, God, *the* perfect and loving Father, wants the best for you and can help you get that best. He wants to help you grow, to be all you can be, to develop strong bonds of relationship with Him, and to grow from level to level in your prayer skills. He is there for us, to teach us, guide us, help us, and just be our Father and intimate Friend. Accept this challenge: if you haven't done so already, first determine at which level you are. Then ask the Lord to help you advance through all the levels of prayer, so that you, too, can have the joy of seeing your potential in prayer reached and your relationship with Him strengthened.

Stretch yourself if you must, but you can expect to see God answer prayer in ways you probably have never imagined were possible. God's power will be released in a greater and mightier way than ever before in your life and in the lives of those for whom you pray. Such results are a part of His promise in John 14:12, that you would do greater things than He. They are a natural result of significant prayer. For example, you may not physically be able to go to the battlefront, but you can be a prayer missionary with just as vital a role in the results as the most seasoned missionary. You help to prepare their way, to intercept and defeat the enemy, to prepare hearts so that they can then go in and reap the harvest of souls. You are their air assault.

As you advance in these levels, you will find more opportunities at church for prayer. Your growth will be an indirect growth in the church family's growth in prayer and in turn the church's prayer life will be strengthened as you are able to use your new skills in praying for church concerns.

When Dwight Eisenhower was being inaugurated president of the United States in January 1953, he surprised the nation by personally offering up a prayer to Almighty God. Here was a man who had commanded three million troops in the invasion of Normandy, was one of the key players in bringing an end to World War II, and now was being inaugurated into the most powerful office in the world. What did he do in front of all the nations of the world and all the people in America? He acknowledged that he needed help. He needed a power greater than he was to fulfill the task before him.

Eisenhower explained: "To the best of my knowledge, the men of courage I have known have been men of faith. I've never seen any of them who weren't."

Dwight Eisenhower understood that God was to be hallowed. Begin by acknowledging who God is. He is all-important in your life.

One of the most striking moments in the 1988 Democratic convention came during a black clergyman's benediction. NBC TV's Connie Chung sought to interview him on camera from the convention floor. "Excuse me, we're praying now," he said to Miss Chung. The press would have to wait. Something far more important than an interview on national television was going on at that time in their history. The Democratic party was acknowledging the power and the presence of God, or at least a segment of it was. Prayer is important because God is important.

Prayer really does change things. You can play a vital role in seeing that change comes about. God is there, eagerly waiting to meet with you, to have fellowship and provide you the guidance and insights He alone can give. That's why God says, "I will build my church…" One of these building blocks definitely, is the strong prayer life of the pastors and leadership which in turn filters to the people. Indeed, the church that is a powerful house of prayer will see proof that the "gates of hell shall not prevail against it" (Matt. 16:18, KJV).

Fire! The smell of smoke recently startled a woman in Austin, Texas. She quickly realized the problem and ran from the house. But then she thought, *I'd better call the fire department so my house doesn't burn down!* Racing back into the house to call 911, she heard the phone ringing. Her boyfriend was on the line. While explaining the emergency to him, she slumped to the ground, overcome by the very problem she was trying to stop. Tragically the flames engulfed her before help could arrive, and she died .

There are times when even believers are like this woman. They smell the "smoke" of the enemy and know there is a problem. Unfortunately, like her, they too often don't recognize the grave danger they are in. They either ignore the problems and hope they will go away, wait too long before acting, or over-analyze the problems and then get into real trouble. No one can afford to wait. The enemy flames are all around. The smoke is getting thicker. Can they call 911? Sure, but it is reached through dialing P.R.A.Y.E.R. God is able to stop whatever the enemy is trying. That is why He assures that "greater is he that is in you than he that is in the world" (1 John 4:4, KJV).

Yes, you see the smoke and sense the strong spiritual warfare around you. By yourself you cannot win, but the Lord is on your side. He wants you to be successful; He has supplied all you need to walk in victory and to be more than overcomers. Your church, when using prayer as God originally intended it, can indeed be a powerful house of prayer!

May your journey toward this goal be one that is taken on God's supersonic jet, not by foot. The time is short. The need so great. The enemy so crafty. Utilize the best, the sharpest weapons in this battle, a battle that can be won, for Jesus has defeated the foe. You are only reclaiming what He has already won at such a great price. Yes, there is a battle, but may you never go into it ill prepared. May you always be fully dressed, using the best weapons and armor available to defeat the enemy and secure God's victory! Both corporately and individually, this is what your Commander and Chief wants and has provided. It is yours for the taking.

Resources

How to Draw Closer to God

Have you ever been so thirsty you thought you couldn't stand it? Your mouth was dry; your body screamed out for water. You wanted water so badly you would have given almost anything for a glass of ice water? In fact you even would have settled for warm water! Just let it be wet!

In Psalm 42:1–2 the psalmist paints just such a picture using a deer who is going through a time of drought. He is so thirsty his tongue probably is hanging out. He uses this illustration to show how much he desires the Lord. He writes, "As the deer pants for streams of water, so my soul pants for you, O God. My soul thirsts for God, for the living God. When can I go and meet with God?" David also expresses this desire in Psalm 63:1.

David was called a man after God's own heart. Isn't it possible that his great longing for God helped to make him this kind of person? Have you ever wanted to be called a person after God's own heart? Someone special to the Lord? You may say, "Yes, but I don't know how to or even if I am able to." Well, there is good news and bad news. The good news is that any believer can be such a person. The bad news isn't really bad—only that it takes time and effort on your part to reach such a place. And prayer is such a key part of getting there. God says in James 4:8 that if we will draw near to Him, then He in turn will draw near to us. So you have to initiate the process. You have to want to draw near to Him and then start to do so. Your heart will be open to the Lord and will be receptive to His drawing closer to you.

But since this is on a spiritual plane, it will be harder to measure your progress. You must not get discouraged if you do not see immediate results. You probably will see results fairly soon, but do not judge the results by the way you feel. Many a person has not reached his or her potential in a skill because the first part of learning it was awkward or uncomfortable. The person was too self-conscious or just plain unable to see any progress. Listen to that future Carnegie Hall pianist as he takes his third or fourth lesson. Ouch! It hurts to listen. But give him time. He's doing well even now, although no one around him but his piano teacher may recognize his progress.

This is how God is with you. He is rooting for you, longing for this close relationship, cheering you on as you start to come toward Him. Like a mother holding out her hands to the baby who is learning to walk, God is with you as you take those "baby steps" toward Him.

So why is drawing close important? Why does it work? For many, one of the important reasons lies in their heart's deepest longing to know God in a deeper, more personal, intimate way. God is so wonderful, loving, kind, and gentle. He cares about you in such a tender way. He is always there for you, and yet sometimes you really are not aware of just how great and wonderful He truly is. Your own imperfect view of Him, often distorted by human relationships and experiences, may have interfered with your getting to know and appreciate Him as He really is.

The concept of drawing nearer to the Lord is a simple one: the closer you come to God, the more you get to know Him, the more your heart is in tune with His. People who are close to the Lord will usually confirm that there are several ways to reach that goal: through pain and suffering; through continual studying of the Word, especially the attributes and works of God; and through opening up their hearts to Him in prayer—in seeking His will, not theirs, in asking to know Him in a deeper, more intimate way. Although the latter is the focus here, often God will use a mixture of all three to draw a person closer to Himself.

One of the best ways to attain this goal is to start looking at God's character qualities, His attributes. As you look at them, in prayer, you can thank Him that He is this way and tell Him how much this means to you in your daily life. This is what David did over and over again in Psalms. He would worship God for His greatness, His power, His goodness, and His workings in his life. Psalms 145 and 150 are such prayers of worship and praise of the Lord. Sometimes David meditated on God's attributes when he was in trouble in order to help him take his eyes off his problems and refocus them on the Lord.

For example, one thing David had learned in this close relationship with the Lord was that he could pour out his heart to the Lord and the Lord would not only hear, but would not criticize him for expressing his concerns, fears, doubts, or questions.

The following excerpt from Psalm 69 is a good example of how God let David pour out his heart, concerns, and frustrations. "Save me, O God, for the waters have come up to my neck. I sink in the miry depths where there is no foothold. I have come into the deep waters; the floods engulf me. I am worn out calling for help; my throat is parched" (vv. 1–3).

The remainder of the psalm tells how David's outlook on things changes as he looks at God and not his circumstances.

Although you may be in the midst of despair, refocus your attention on the Lord in prayer and in recalling His character your spirits will be lifted as you get His perspective on the problem you are facing.

In the psalms David uses such phrases as, "My soul clings to You" and "Your right hand upholds me" (63:8).

The following is a sample prayer for a person who is sensing a struggle in his or her prayer life. One can pray it as is, or adapt it according to the situation and feelings.

Father, I feel a coldness in my times with You, as if I have lost my first love. I want to know You better, to feel Your presence, to draw nearer to Your heart. But I have to admit, I feel a dullness in my spirit, a barrier in my emotions. I just can't seem to break through to You. Please remove whatever is keeping me from being as I once was. Show me what I need to do. Oh, my Father, let me come and sit on Your lap, feel Your arms around me, and sense Your pleasure in me, Your acceptance of me just as I am. Let this knowledge go deep into my heart, into my emotions. Flood me with You. Give me a fresh awareness of You and how wonderful You are. Overflow my soul with joy that comes from our sweet relationship. Soften my heart so I am like a child before You, open and vulnerable. I love You so much.

Make a list of goals you would like to reach in your prayer time—how long you would like to pray (how much now and how much ultimately); things you would like to be able to do (deeper intercession, drawing closer to God, understanding His will and heart on things); becoming more like Jesus; having your emotions more deeply involved in expressing your love to Him; and going from one level of intercession (see p. 7 and chap. 9) to the next ones.

Recognize that each of these goals may take some time to realize. Don't set unrealistic time frames which might cause you to get discouraged. Be flexible. Focus on how much the Lord is doing in your life already, rather than all that needs to be done. Take your steps in bite sizes.

Going through resource 2 is a good step in this process. Be certain to include the love letter to the Lord by journaling (resource 19, sample #3). It will be very helpful. Also, check out some of the ideas in resource 16.

Two-Week Enrichment

The following is a suggested outline for fourteen days of quiet times with the Lord. It is designed to help you draw closer to Him, to broaden your prayer skills, and to give you a variety of patterns to help keep your prayer times fresh and meaningful with Him. Some of it draws on materials found in the resources of this book.

For those who have the time and desire, there are several books you could start reading. Begin with the one that appeals most to you.

Suggestions

- *Touch the World Through Prayer* by Wesley Duewell. It gives a good overall view of prayer and can help increase vision.
- *With Christ in the School of Prayer* by Andrew Murray is a long-time favorite of many. It gives you the heart for prayer and communication with Him. (More focused than Duewell.)
- *Quiet Talks on Prayer* by S. D. Gordon also is a classic.
- *Praying Hyde* by Francis McGraw is a small but powerful book to increase vision and faith in what God can do through one insignificant person who starts praying in earnest.

For persons more experienced in prayer:

- *Intimate Friendship with God* by Joy Dawson is an excellent book.
- *The God Who Hears* by John Hunter probes questions and problems you may face in prayer and looks at the attributes which answers these problems.

- *Too Busy Not to Pray* by Bill Hybles challenges a person to examine his/her attitude toward prayer and slow down enough to have a meaningful time with God.
- *Worship His Majesty* by Jack Hayford and *Majesty* by J. Sidlow are both books which will help you appreciate and worship God in a deeper way.

See resource 4 for further ideas.

Overview for Each Day

Even though you may not be a great writer, you will be asked to write your responses to the Lord in a love letter format. (See resource 19, sample #3.)

Several steps will be taken each day as you go through these fourteen days. First, you will worship God in general and then for a specific attribute, a different one each day. As part of your worship, you will record ways you have seen that attribute in operation, especially in your own life and the lives of those who are close to you. Notice in the samples that this is done in a conversational manner, not just a listing out of things. The more your time is in a conversational style, the more you will be able to break down the wall of formalness that too often keeps us at arms length from our Friend.

The questions on each attribute are designed to help you better appreciate the importance of God possessing each of His attributes. Often times, looking at God causes us to see our own sin. A time is included for self-searching of the last twenty-four hours along with questions about specific sins.

Next, you will focus on a specific element or type of prayer. In focusing on that element, you will be praying for your own specific concerns and those of your family, friends, or church.

Each day includes a time to thank the Lord specifically for what He has done in the last twenty-four hours. Verses for meditation and to claim are given for various areas along with a suggested Scripture passage. You should also spend time listening to the Lord and writing out what He has said. Close with giving your day to the Lord and a time of praise.

The fourteen days are designed to have variety in the content of each prayer time. The more variety there is, the less chance for boredom or losing interest.

Naturally, you may add to each day whatever other things are on your heart. But this gives you a new approach and a foundation on which to add any other materials you wish to bring to the Lord.

As you start each day, you may want to orally say something like the following:

Father, Today, as I talk with You, I ask that first of all this place be a holy of holies for You and me where nothing else is allowed to interfere. May only Your Spirit speak to me during this time.

NOTE: *Everyday you will want to pray for the following:*

- Praise
- Self-examination to recognize any unconfessed sin.
- Family members (at least one per day). Pray Scripture qualities for them from such passages as Colossians 1:9,12,23; Philippians 1:9–11; Ephesians 3:16–19; 2 Timothy 1:7. (See resource 16i.)
- Pastor, church leadership. (See resource 16a.)
- Thanksgiving for His help in the previous day. Be specific.
- Give your day to the Lord. Ask for His control and guidance. Be specific if there are certain things you know you need His help with.
- Put on the armor of God. (See resource 3A.)

Each person will take a different amount of time to complete the suggested amount. Try to do every part of the day's experiment, but if time will not allow you to or you are struggling too much, then *do what you can.* Your goal should be to do it all, so if you are having problems, try to do a little more each day so that you work your way up to a larger chunk of time.

Above all, don't let it become a burden or put you on a guilt trip. Ask the Lord to change you, to help you have a heart that desires this more than anything else. (See sample prayer in resource 1.) Thank Him that He is in the process of changing you because this is your heart's desire and is consistent with what He wants. Claim the promise of 1 John 5:14–15.

Try journaling your prayers in a loose-leaf notebook and in a love letter format. Do this especially in the praise, worship, and thanksgiving sections. (See resource 19, sample #3.) Date each day's writing. Requests can also be journaled, but daily ones might take too long for the busy person. It is also an excellent way to keep focused, on track and to have more accountability. (Prayerworks has an excellent booklet on how to have a personal prayer journal. See resource 4, "Prayer in the Church," for address.)

Consider putting marks in your loose-leaf notebook. You may want to put an arrow on the left-hand side of the page at any point you want to remember. An M also could indicate a verse you want to memorize later. Using different colored ink also is helpful, especially if you write down a verse in red so you can easily find it later. Green ink could denote someone else's materials you found helpful and have copied. Your heart's response to both the Scriptures and these other materials could be in another color.

If you do not have a regular plan for reading the Scriptures, start in Psalms. Read one psalm per day, using the day that corresponds with the month (i.e., on the first day of the month read Ps. 1; the second day Ps. 2, etc.). On the thirty-first day, read something else or review the verses that you have marked in the last month that have been so meaningful. For the next month, you will start with Psalm 31; the second day, Psalm 32, etc.

In five months you will read all of Psalms. You may also want to add a New Testament reading depending on your time. In all your reading, it is helpful to underline and make notes as well as record in your love letter what the Lord is saying to you.

For those who are more advanced or would like to do so, make an attribute notebook in which you have a loose-leaf notebook. Title each page with a single attribute (love, good, faithful, Provider, Counselor, etc.). Then, as you find a verse that includes that attribute *and* means something to you, write it out fully on the page. (One verse may be appropriate for more than one attribute, so write it on each page.) In a different color ink you may want to put down any response emotionally you have, or comments or ideas about it.

You may also want to do the same thing for Emotions/Concepts like fear, worry, guidance, anger, or lust. In a similar fashion, write out verses pertaining to these words. Also add any personal example(s) of where that attribute has been exhibited by God in your life or that of a friend. You may also want to write down things you read that are appropriate thoughts on the subject from such places as a devotional book, sermon, or something you hear or read.

When you are having a rough day or problems, look to your attribute or emotion page that would cover your problem. For example, when you are having financial problems, look to the one entitled "Provider." Reading this material can encourage you and increase your faith when it comes under attack.

On days you are facing serious problems or difficulties, focus your time on one or more of God's attributes that will meet or solve that situation. Do this before you bring the problem to Him.

You should find the problem seems less severe after focusing on the God who has the ability to solve it.

The first four days have a "Prayer Focus" which present the A.C.T.S method of praying (Adoration, Confession, Thanksgiving, Supplication). This is a simple acrostic to help you remember the different elements in prayer.

Prayer Focus: Adoration. Tell the Lord how much you appreciate Him because of His great love for you. Mention ways in which He has shown His love recently and in the past. (Ps. 86:8–13)

Day One

Attribute Focus: Loving (John 3:16; 15:13; 1 John 4:16). Questions and interactions on this attribute:

• Is it important that God is loving? Why?

• What would God be like if He were not loving and how would that change my relationship and/or confidence in Him? Tell Him how this makes you feel. Confident? Secure? Special? Accepted?

• How have I seen God's love displayed in my life?

Self-examination: Ask the Lord to show you anything that is unloving or displeasing to Him in your life, or that still needs to be confessed. Claim 1 John 1:9. If necessary go to any person with whom you need to make things right. The following prayer can be adapted to use in dealing with certain sins.

> Dear Father, You know I have a problem with _____. I know this is displeasing to You and hurts You. I don't want to _____, yet as much as I have tried to stop, I have been too weak to stop permanently. I give up. If I am ever going to stop, You are going to have to give me the power to stop. So I am asking You, Holy Spirit, to remind me the next time I am about to _____. Show me what I have to do to resist this sin and then give me the courage to do so. I believe I am asking according to Your will. Therefore I claim Your promise in 1 John 5:14–15 that You will answer yes to my request. Thank You that I will be victorious in this. I believe, Lord. Help my unbelief.

Sometimes you know something is wrong but just can't bring yourself to let loose of it. In that case, you need to pray a "pre-prayer" of repentance similar to the following:

> Father, You know I have a weakness, a sin of _____ I just cannot give up at this time. I know it is wrong and hurts You, but I am too weak to stop. In some ways I'm scared to stop. I fear the conse-

quences of stopping. But I love You so much, I don't want anything to be between us. I am now giving You permission to give me the desire to give it up. Help me fully to trust You in this area, as difficult as I know that may be. I certainly know I will never be able to stop without Your help, so I'm asking for it now. Thank You that You want this so much more than I do and that You will change my desires. I love and trust You.

Thanksgiving for His Help: Thank the Lord for His help in the previous day. Be specific. Thank Him for His great salvation and all it cost Him.

Family: Pray for one or more family members, their needs, claim verses for them, protection, etc. In resource 16i there are several different compilations of prayers you can use such as praying character qualities or praying for a difficult person, for salvation, etc. Even better is to make a similar one tailor-made for the person and his or her needs.

Specific Concern: Relations with neighbors. Their salvation/ growth in the Lord. Any problems they are facing.

Other Concerns: Am I always loving to others?

Scripture Reading: Your choice or Psalm 1.

What I Sense the Lord is Saying to Me: Write down whatever the Lord may be showing you. (Am I showing/modeling this attribute of God to others? Is there something I need to correct? To add to my activities?) Do this at whatever point(s) He shows you something.

Put on God's Armor; Give Myself and My Day to Him: Put on the armor of God, preferably out loud. (See resource 3a.) Be certain to ask the Lord to help you keep every thought under His control, to be able to recognize the voice and attacks of the enemy, and to resist them in His power. Ask that He be glorified in this day. Give your time to the Lord, trusting that if something interferes with *your* schedule, that *He* has something better to do with your time for that part of your day. Ask for His peace to rule your day.

Closing Thanks and Praise: Close with a time of worshiping the Lord. You may use something from the Scriptures (especially the psalms), or simply express what is in your heart. You can also express your thanks for all He has and is doing for you, what you are learning, how you are feeling toward Him and others, positive changes you are seeing, and His faithfulness, to mention a few.

Day Two   *Prayer Focus:* Confession. Turn to resource 13 and look at the list of hindrances to prayer. Ask the Lord to point out any that are standing between you and Him. Confess any He shows you. If this is a habitual sin, ask Him to show you how to overcome this permanently by drawing on His power to have the victory. (See resource 7 for sample prayer and an expansion on this truth.) (Isa. 59:1–2)

Attribute Focus: Forgiving (Ps. 103:3; Ps. 86:5). Questions and interactions on this attribute:

- Is it important that God is forgiving Why?
- What if God only forgave certain sins and not others? Or I never knew which ones He would or would not forgive? What would I feel?
- How would this affect my ability to be close to Him? Tell Him how this makes you feel and thank Him for His full forgiveness of all your sins.
- Where have I recently experienced His forgiveness?

Self-examination: Is there any unconfessed sin? Any unforgiveness of family members, parents, teachers, friends, work colleagues, or neighbors? (Matt. 5:23–24) (See resource 5.)

Thanksgiving for His Help: Thank the Lord for His help in the previous day, for good health, and for you and family.

Family...

Specific Concern: Mayor and City Council (or other appropriate service/governmental agencies). (Prov. 11:11; 15:33; 16:9; 21:1–3)

Other Concerns...

Scripture Reading: Your choice or Psalm 2.

What I Sense the Lord Is Saying to Me...

Put on God's Armor; Give Myself and My Day to Him...

Closing Thanks and Praise...

Prayer Focus: Thanksgiving. Thanksgiving for what He has done in creation, in providing salvation, and in all the various aspects of your life that would be disasters without His help. Also include thanks for His help in the previous day. (Ps. 95:2; 107:22)   **Day Three**

Attribute Focus: Faithful, dependable, unchangeable (Lam. 3:22, 23; Jas. 1:17; Heb. 13:8; 1 Cor. 10:13; 1 Thess. 5:24). Questions and interactions on these attributes:

- Is it important that God is faithful, dependable and unchangeable? Why?

- Could I feel secure if I knew that at times He would change and not be dependable?
- How would this affect my confidence level in Him, especially in times of trouble?
- Can I depend upon His promises to me, that He will faithfully keep them?
- Where have I seen His faithfulness in my life? Express your appreciation for these aspects of His nature and tell Him how they make you feel.

Self-examination: Is there any unconfessed sin? Is my behavior or attitude in any way doubting His faithfulness, dependability or unchangeable nature? Any anger or harsh words spoken? (Prov. 15:1; Eccl. 6:9; Jas. 3)

Family...

Specific Concern: An item in the news that concerns you.

Other Concerns...

Scripture Reading: Your choice or Psalm 3.

What I Sense the Lord Is Saying to Me...

Put on God's Armor; Give Myself and My Day to Him...

Closing Thanks and Praise...

Day Four *Attribute focus:* Guide (Ps. 32:8; Isa. 48:17). Questions and interactions on this attribute:

- Is it important that God is my guide? Why?
- What would my life be like if I couldn't have God's guidance?
- What if He were willing to guide me, but was not always trustworthy or loving or did not know everything or was not perfect?
- How would I feel about any guidance He offered under those circumstances? Tell the Lord how important it is to you that you can receive His expert guidance.
- Where have I seen God's guidance recently in my life?

Self-examination: Is there any unconfessed sin? Is there any way I am rejecting or not seeking God's guidance in my life? Any critical spirit? (Eph. 4:1–3; Phil. 2:1–4,14)

Thanksgiving for His Help: Thank the Lord for His help on the previous day, for His provision.

Prayer Focus: Supplication. (Note: supplication is in two parts—(a.) intercession for others and (b.) requests for myself) Using resource 16, choose one or more helps to intercede for a family member and for one person in leadership at church. (Note: this time the prayer focus is not at the first because whenever possible in our quiet times, worship in some form should always precede our prayers.)

Family (You may have already covered this in the previous section.)...

Specific Concern: President of the United States, Congress (1 Tim. 2:1; Prov. 2:2–6; 14:34; 15:33; 16:9; 21:1–3).

Other Concerns...

Scripture Reading: Your choice or Psalm 4.

What I Sense the Lord Is Saying to Me...

Put on God's Armor; Give Myself and My Day To Him...

Closing Thanks and Praise...

Attribute Focus: Holy, pure, righteous (1 Pet. 1:16). Questions and interactions on this attribute: **Day Five**

- Is it important that God is holy, pure, and righteous? Why?
- How would I feel if He were sinful like me, or impure?
- What would this mean about my salvation?
- Could I accept for an unholy God to judge me?
- How would His unrighteousness impact my worship of Him?
- Where have I seen God's holiness, purity, and righteousness?

Self examination: Is there any unconfessed sin? Any compromise of God's standards and values?

Prayer Focus: Request. A closer, deeper walk with God. (Ps. 42:1. See resource 1.)

Thanksgiving for His help: Thank the Lord for His help in the previous day and for the convicting of the Holy Spirit
Family...

Specific Concern: Pastor and his family; church leadership (See resource 16a for list of requests.)

Other Concerns...

Scripture Reading: Your choice or Psalm 5.

What I Sense the Lord Is Saying to Me...

Put on God's Armor; Give Myself and My Day to Him...

Closing Thanks and Praise...

Attribute Focus: Patience (Num. 14:18; Ps. 86:15; 2 Pet. 3:9). **Day Six**
Questions and interactions on this attribute:

- Is it important that God is patient? Why?
- How would I feel when I made a mistake if I knew God was not always patient?
- Would this change my sense of security and trust?
- How have I seen God's patience with me?

Self-examination: Is there any unconfessed sin? Any dishonesty? Lying? Shading the truth? Am I a patient person? (Ps. 63:1; Prov. 30:8)

Thanksgiving for His Help: Thank the Lord for His help in the previous day. Recall a difficult decision in the past in which you saw His guidance. Thank Him for it.
Family...

Specific Concern: Media—TV, Hollywood, newspapers, magazines (Phil. 4:8; Prov. 2:2–6).

Other Concerns...

Scripture Reading: Your choice or Psalm 6.

What I Sense the Lord Is Saying to Me...

Put on God's Armor; Give Myself and My Day to Him...

Closing Thanks and Praise...

Day Seven   *Attribute Focus:* Friend, Companion (Prov. 18:24; Matt. 11:19; John 15:14; Heb. 13:5).
Questions and interactions on this attribute:

- Is it important that God is my Friend and Companion?
- Do I trust God as a close Friend and Companion?
- Do I have this level of relationship with Him? Why/why not?
- What if He said He were my Friend but changed all the time, was undependable, dishonest with me? Could I truly draw close to Him?
- Is our friendship based on my behavior or something else? Tell the Lord what you think about His friendship and being your companion.

Self-examination: Is there any unconfessed sin? Are there any barriers keeping our relationship from being all God wants it to be? Am I treating the "temple of God" well? Any addictive behavior (drugs, pornography, gambling, etc.)? (Phil. 4:8; 1 Pet. 5:8)

Thanksgiving for His Help: Thank the Lord for His help in the previous day, for always being there for you and with you, and for your job.

Family...

Specific Concern: Educational system (curriculum, teachers, administrators, school board). (Ps. 34:11; Prov. 2:2–6; Col. 2:8)

Other Concerns...

What I Sense the Lord Is Saying to Me...

Scripture Reading: Your choice or Psalm 7.

Put on God's Armor; Give Myself and My Day to Him...

Closing Thanks and Praise...

Attribute Focus: Majestic, Glorious, Awesome (Ex. 15:11; Neh. 9:32; Ps. 76:4).   **Day Eight**

Questions and interactions on this attribute:

- Is it important that God is majestic, glorious, and awesome? Why?
- Does this enhance my ability to worship Him?
- What if He looked just like man? Would He seem like God to me as I understand Him today?
- Do I have a good perspective of God's glory and majesty, or has He been distorted by my human relationships or unfounded fears of Him?

Self-examination: Is there any unconfessed sin? Any sexual sin either physically or in my mind? (2 Cor. 10:3–5; Phil. 4:8. See day 1 of this category for prayer.)

Thanksgiving for His Help: Thank the Lord for His help in the previous day, and for your gifting and His teaching you how to use it and giving you opportunities to do so.

Family...

Specific Concern: Governor of state and Legislature. (Ps. 2:10,11; Prov. 21:3)

Other Concerns...

Scripture Reading: Your choice or Psalm 8.

What I Sense the Lord Is Saying to Me...

Put on God's Armor; Give Myself and My Day to Him...

Closing Thanks and Praise...

Attribute Focus: All powerful (Jer. 32:17, 26; Matt. 28:18).   **Day Nine**

Questions and interactions on this attribute:

- Is it important that God has all power? Why?
- What if He were all powerful but were not all knowing? Or were not present everywhere and might not be aware of my current problem?

- Could I trust Him to work everything out together for good?
- What if He had certain limits on His power?
- In what ways have I experienced God's power in my life?

Self-examination: Is there any unconfessed sin? Any habit I cannot break? How can God's power be applied specifically to these weaknesses? Am I letting Him? Am I *willing* to let Him? (See day 1 of this category for prayer.)

Thanksgiving for His Help: Thank God for His help on the previous day and for the changes He is making in your life. *Family...*

Specific Concern: Missionaries (especially those from your church) and the unsaved. (Eph. 6:3; 2 Tim. 2:24,25;/ Rom. 10:1; 1 Tim. 2:1,3,4)

Other Concerns...

Scripture Reading: Your choice or Psalm 9.

What I Sense the Lord Is Saying to Me...

Put on God's Armor; Give Myself and My Day to Him...

Closing Thanks and Praise...

Day Ten *Attribute Focus:* Peace Giver (John 14:27; 2 Thess. 3:16). Questions and interactions on this attribute:

- Is it important that God is a giver of peace? Why?
- What if He withheld His peace when I asked for it? Or never gave it?
- What if I had to go through difficult times without His peace?
- In what ways have I experienced God's peace when I should have been upset?

Self examination: Is there any unconfessed sin? Do I worry about things and not fully trust the Lord? What things or wrong thinking do I allow to take God's peace from me? (Prov. 3:5–7; 1 Pet. 5:7) What do I need to stop worrying or fretting about now?

Thanksgiving for His Help: Thank the Lord for His help in the previous day and for the sense of security you feel because He is there to help you, to be there for you always.

Family...

Specific Concern: Morality in our nation (Prov. 14:34; Phil. 4:8).

Other Concerns...

Scripture Reading: Your choice or Psalm 10.

What I Sense the Lord Is Saying to Me...

Put on God's Armor; Give Myself and My Day to Him...

Closing Thanks and Praise...

Attribute Focus: Wise, having all knowledge (Job 21:22; Job 38; 39; 1 Tim. 1:17). Questions and interactions on this attribute: **Day Eleven**

- Is it important that God is wise and has all knowledge? Why?
- What if He only had partial knowledge?
- How much could I trust His leading? Or how much could I trust His promise in Romans 8:28?
- What if He didn't use His knowledge with wisdom?
- Where have I seen God's wisdom in my life?

Self-examination: Is there any unconfessed sin? Have I been acting with my own wisdom and not seeking God's in everything? Do I mistrust God's wisdom when I read a "hard saying" in the Word? (Prov. 2:1–6; 3:5–7; Rom. 12:6). Am I resisting any of His wisdom right now?

Thanksgiving for His Help: Thank the Lord for His help in the previous day and for showing you a good church in which to worship.

Family...

Specific Concern: Justice system (Supreme Court, federal and state, and local). (Ex. 18:21–22a; Deut. 16:18; Ps. 2:10,11; Ps. 82:2–4).

Other Concerns...

Scripture Reading: Your choice or Psalm 11.

What I Sense the Lord Is Saying to Me...

Put on God's Armor; Give Myself and My Day to Him...

Closing Thanks and Praise ...

Attribute Focus: Gracious, compassionate (Neh. 9:31; Heb. 4:15). Questions and interactions on this attribute: **Day Twelve**

- Is it important that God is gracious and compassionate? Why?
- What if He were brash, uncaring, crude, rude, abrupt?
- Would I be able to draw close to Him, to want His attention? Could He make me feel accepted just as I am?
- Do I ever doubt God's graciousness and compassion to me?

- Where have I seen God's graciousness and compassion in my life?

Self-examination: Have I been humble before the Lord? Do I ever take credit for what He has done in and through me? Am I puffed up? Impressed with myself and my abilities? (Jer. 9:23; 1 Cor. 4:7; Jas. 4:6; 1 Pet. 5:5,6)

Thanksgiving for His Help: Thank the Lord for His help in the previous day and for helping you learn over the years how to interact more successfully with people.

Family...

Specific Concern: Unity in the church, especially in my own church and between the churches in my city. (Ps. 133:1; John 17:11, 20–23; Eph. 4:1–3; Phil. 2:1–4, 14; 2 Tim. 2:14, 23–25).

Other Concerns...

Scripture Reading: Your choice or Psalm 12.

What I Sense the Lord Is Saying to Me...

Put on God's Armor; Give Myself and My Day to Him...

Closing Thanks and Praise...

Day Thirteen *Attribute Focus:* Protector. (Ps. 27:1–5; 101) Questions and interactions on this attribute:

- Is it important that God is my protector? Why?
- What if God did not want to protect me all the time? How would I feel the next time I was in jeopardy or danger?
- What if He wanted to protect me 100 percent of the time, but did not have all power to do so or was not present everywhere to know when I needed protection?
- How do I feel knowing He is protecting me?

Self-examination: Is there any unconfessed sin? Am I a fearful person? Do I fear God cannot protect me in a certain area? Am I trusting God for *every* detail of my life? What attribute(s) of God could answer my fears? (Prov. 3:5–10; Heb. 13:5,6; 2 Tim. 1:7; 1 Pet. 5:7; 1 John 4:18).

Thanksgiving for His Help: Thank the Lord for His help in the previous day and for giving you the ability to enjoy His creation (eyes, ears, smell, touch and an appreciation for color, sizes, shapes, variety).

Family...

Specific Concern: The youth of our nation (morality, salvation, drugs, gangs, peer group, obey parents). (Ps. 34:11; Phil. 4:8; Col. 2:8; 2 Tim. 2:22)

Other Concerns...

Scripture Reading: Your choice or Psalm 13.

What I Sense the Lord Is Saying to Me...

Put on God's Armor; Give Myself and My Day to Him...

Closing Thanks and Praise...

Attribute Focus: Comforter (John 14:6; 2 Cor. 1:3). Questions and interactions on this attribute:

Day Fourteen

- Is it important that God is my Comforter? Why?
- How would I feel if He never offered comfort in my trouble?
- What if He wanted to comfort me, but didn't have all knowledge or wasn't present everywhere and therefore sometimes missed my hurts?

Self-examination: Is there any unconfessed sin? Is there any area I am not letting God be my Comforter? Am I discontent, a complainer? (Phil. 2:14; 4:11)

Thanksgiving for His help: Thank the Lord for His help in the previous day and for safety.

Family...

Specific Concern: Christian religious leaders (true to the Word and teach it with authority, morally pure and a good example to all, guided by the Lord, humble, fear God more than man, endure the hardships of ministry). Resource 16a has more ideas. (1 Cor. 4:2, 6b; 2 Tim. 2:3, 10, 15, 16; 4:2)

Other Concerns...

Scripture Reading: Your choice or Psalm 14.

What I Sense the Lord Is Saying to Me...

Put on God's Armor; Give Myself and My Day to Him...

Closing Thanks and Praise...

Now that you have completed these fourteen days, you may want to branch out on your own or simply go through these again. Include the following attributes of God and others as you come across those that are meaningful to you or you want to explore: good, honest, truthful, Savior, kind, gentle, relational, Father. You may also want to study the different Hebrew and Greek names of God for a more in-depth study of His attributes.

   One final note: This is in no way meant to be an exhaustive study. It only sets some guidelines to get you started. You will have the joy of discovering so many more verses, more angles of things to pray for and different approaches to the same topic. You may enjoy keeping a notebook of ideas. Be creative! That is one of the gifts God has given you for great joy when you use it. How appropriate to use it in drawing closer to Him.

The Armor of God

You are in a daily battle whether you know it or not. That is why in Ephesians 6 you are told to "put on the full armor of God" (v. 11). Just as a soldier gets dressed each day, Christians need to put on our spiritual clothing each morning. But for many, putting on the armor of God has become a routine akin to a magical incantation and similar to how some pray the Lord's Prayer. Instead it should be a well-thought-out, purposeful process which helps prepare you for whatever may come in your day. The difference between the two lies in what you are thinking as you "put on the armor."

Become familiar with this armor before you put it on. First of all, you may have noticed that all the elements of the armor and what they represent are actually describing the nature of Jesus. For example, He is our salvation, righteousness, and peace. He is truth and the Word of God. Most of the armor is a protection, a covering of the vital parts of your body, so when the enemy attacks, he cannot touch you. You may not stop the attack, but you can stop any wounding. The sword is your only truly offensive piece. But, oh, how powerful it is! When you skillfully combine the Word of God (the sword) with faith (the shield), you have an unbeatable protection against whatever attacks the enemy may hurl at you during your day's "battle."

For ease of memory, put on the armor from top to bottom. The following sections are suggested prayer for putting on your armor each morning before you go out. You will find that several parts of the prayer go somewhat beyond the standard "putting on" since they are scriptural extensions of the basics of each piece of armor. Feel free to adapt this to fit your particular way of expressing yourself and the needs of your day's agenda.

Helmet of Salvation

Understanding Its Purpose: There are three tenses of "salvation": past, present, and future. You already are saved from the *penalty* of sin (past). In your present you need salvation from the *power* of sin which is what the helmet is for. In the future you will be saved from the *presence* of sin. The helmet covers your mind.

All sin of any kind originates in the mind: rebellion, lying, lust, murder, rejection of God, wrong thoughts, etc. Your words are spoken only after they have gone through your mind. Therefore, if you can keep all of your thoughts under Jesus' control, commanded in 2 Corinthians 10:3–5, then sin will have no power over you. In other words, it won't have a chance to get a foothold because you will have successfully resisted the temptation as you've brought that negative thought under the Saviour's control.

This means you need to first recognize the enemy's temptation, expose the lie he is telling you, and reject thinking about it any more. Often times the Lord will bring Scripture to your mind (the sword) to help in this process. *Note:* Often the enemy's lies can be recognized by the fact that they cause you to think negatively about yourself—helpless, in despair, like a victim, even suicidal—or others (he is the accuser of the brethren).

Another tactic he uses is to make you question God's goodness; His power, ability, or desire to help you; or your worthiness of being helped by Him. Thoughts like, *If God really loved me, He wouldn't have let _____ happen.* Or *God really doesn't care about me very much. How could He? Look at what I've done. I've always been bad, weak, a failure, [etc.]*

Sample Prayer:

I put on the helmet of salvation for You, Lord, to protect me today from the power of sin. Keep the enemy from successfully tempting me in any way. Help me, Holy Spirit, to keep every thought under the control of the Lord Jesus. Help me today to recognize the temptations and lies of the enemy every time he tries to trick me or get me to believe a half truth or be suspicious of someone. Let me think only Your thoughts. Control my tongue so that I speak only Your words. Let my words be edifying (positive and building up) to everyone. Let me only speak the truth and to do so in Your love. Conform my will to Yours so that I only do what You want me to this day.

Lord, I put on Your righteousness to protect me in all I do this day. Let everything I do be done in a right way. Let me be squeaky clean in all I do, say, or think. Let me walk in Your righteousness and not try to walk in my own righteousness. Holy Spirit, show me any time I am trying to live in my own goodness, strength and abilities rather than Yours.	Breastplate of Righteousness
Lord Jesus, You are Truth. I therefore put on truth to cover every act, every expression, every word I say. Help me not to compromise or shade the truth in any way. Let Your truths be foundational to all I do this day.	Belt of Truth
Father, I need the peace of Jesus to saturate all my day, to be part of everything I do and say. I need His peace in my mind, no matter what the situation. As I look at You and not the situation, let Your peace rule my heart and mind. Thank You that You will help me to walk in peace throughout my day. I am available to share Your peace with anyone with whom You want me to do so.	Shoes of the Gospel of Peace
Help me to use my shield of faith in a strong, effective way today to stop all of the enemy's fiery darts in whatever form they may take. As You show me his temptations, help me to use my faith to resist and quench his attempts to make me doubt You or to view myself or others in a negative way. Cause my faith to be strengthened as I use it and as I see You and who You are in each and every situation I encounter. Bring to my mind appropriate verses to help quench every fiery dart of the wicked one. Let Your Word be a sharp instrument in my mouth to come against all the lies and deceptions of the enemy.	Shield of Faith, Sword of the Spirit

Father, as I walk through this day, let me walk in confidence that I am prepared for this day's battle, for I have on my armor. More importantly I know that You who indwell me are greater than he who is in the world and is my enemy. Help me to remember that he is a defeated foe, and although he roars as a lion, his teeth have been pulled—he has no ability to touch me apart from Your permission. I am a victorious soldier in this warfare today because of who I am in Jesus and who He is in me. Thank You for the great confidence that gives me to face all this day will hold. I place this day in Your hands and give You permission to change my plans for this day in whatever way You see fit. May You be glorified in all I say and do this day.

How to Close the Holes In Your Armor

- Pray. Pray. Pray.
- Recognize that the (weakness) hole is there.
- Discover what area of God's nature you are not trusting in. (Inevitably involved in this hole is a lack of faith in God's ability.)
- Try to see in what ways the enemy attacks you; i.e., when are you vulnerable to his attacks, what sets it off, and how are you failing to trust God in this area.
- Confess the weakness as sin and ask forgiveness from God and, where appropriate, anyone you have offended.
- Ask the Lord to give you appropriate Scripture to claim that will strengthen that area and resist the enemy's attack.
- Request the Lord's help in bringing every thought under His control. Use 2 Corinthians 10:5 as your foundation to do this.
- Seek the Lord's help to strengthen your faith to understand which of His characteristics and promises are applicable to this weakness. Be certain to claim the truth of Philippians 4:13, "I can do all things through Him who strengthens me" (NASB).

Annotated Bibliography

The following books are only a sample of the rich literature available on prayer. It is not meant to be a comprehensive listing and may not have your favorite book, but each book mentioned is well worth reading. Unfortunately, space does not permit to list all books available on a subject or to have descriptions of each.

Some of these books may not be in print but are well worth tracking down in used books stores. Note also that although the value of the complete content of some books may be open to interpretation, there is helpful material for churches and individuals in each of these books.

Awaken the Dawn. Earnest B. Gentile. San Jose, Calif.: Bible Temple Publishing, 1990; 1-800-777-6057. Good material for developing your own personal quiet time.

Could You Not Tarry One Hour? Larry Lea. Altamonte Springs, Fla.: Creation House, 1987. Uses the Lord's Prayer as a format for spending an hour in prayer.

Handle with Prayer. Charles F. Stanley. Wheaton, Ill.: Victor Books, 1986. Learning prayer principles, including avoiding enemy attacks, praying while waiting, how to pray the will of God, and effective intercession.

Releasing God's Power (hardback name), *Let Prayer Change Your Life* (paperback name). Becky Tirabassi. Nashville, Tenn.: Oliver Nelson Books (hardback), Thomas Nelson (paperback), 1990. Paperback version has added a thirteen-week study guide.

The Necessity of Prayer. E.M. Bounds. Grand Rapids, Mich.: Baker Book House, 1976. A classic on various factors in prayer as well as the mystery and majesty of prayer.

The Prayer Factor. Sammy Tippit. Chicago, Ill.: Moody Press, 1988. This book helps establish a consistent, effective prayer life by

General Teachings/Quiet Time Helps

understanding the gift and power of prayer. Also has section on role of prayer in spiritual awakening.

Prayers that Avail Much (also *Volume Two*). Word Ministries, Inc. Tulsa, Okla.: Harrison House, 1980, (1989). Intercessor's handbook of scriptural prayers.

Touching the Heart of God. Leonard E. LeSourd, ed. Old Tappan, N.J.: 1990 Chosen Books A compilation of stirring testimonies and clear teaching from a host of the world's foremost "prayer warriors" in ten categories, including when you don't know how to pray, praying for those you don't know, learning to listen, overcoming obstacles, spiritual warfare, does prayer change God's mind, scriptural praying, igniting the church, intercession in action. They also have a *companion workbook* you can get to help you think through and interact more with the material. Designed to be an eleven-week course for group or private study.

With Christ in the School of Prayer. Andrew Murray. Old Tappan, N.J.: Revell, 1953. A classic. Must reading.

YWAM Prayer Diary. Youth with a Mission. Diary and prayer guide for covering the world in a year. Frontline Communications, P.O. Box 55787, Seattle, WA 98155.

All the Prayers of the Bible. Herbert Lockger. Grand Rapids, Mich.: Zondervan, 1980.

How to Develop a Praying Church. Charlie Shedd. Nashville, Tenn: Abingdon Press, 1964.

Lord, Teach Us to Pray. Alexander Whyte. Grand Rapids, Mich.: Baker Book House, 1976.

Mighty Prevailing Prayer. Wesley Duewel. Grand Rapids, Mich.: Zondervan, 1990.

Power Through Prayer. E.M. Bounds. Chicago, Ill.: Moody Press, 1979.

Prayer. O. Hallesby. Minneapolis, Minn.: Augsburg Publishing House, 1959. A classic.

Prayer: Finding the Heart's True Home. Richard J. Foster. San Francisco, Calif.: Harper Collins, 1992.

Prayer for Those Who Influence Your Family. Prayerworks. 38-00 Arrowhead Springs, San Bernardino, CA 92414.

Prayer Ministry in the Local Church. Steve Harper. Grand Rapids, Mich.: Baker Book House, 1976.

Prayer, the Mightiest Force in the World. Frank C. Lauback. Old Tappan, N.J.: Revell, 1959.

Prayer Power Unlimited. J. Oswald Sanders. Minneapolis, Minn.: World Wide Publications, 1977.

Prevailing Prayer. D.L. Moody. Chicago, Ill.: Moody Press, n.d.

Principles of Prayer. Charles G. Finney. Minneapolis, Minn.: Bethany Fellowship, Inc., 1980.

Purpose in Prayer. E.M. Bounds. Grand Rapids, Mich.: Baker Book House, 1978.

Quiet Talks on Prayer. Samuel D. Gordon. New York, N.Y.: Grosset and Dunlap, 1904.

Something Happens When Churches Pray. Warren Wiersbe. Lincoln, Neb.: Back to the Bible, 1984.

The Kneeling Christian. Author unknown. Grand Rapids, Mich.: Zondervan, 1986.

The Power of Positive Praying. John Bisagno. Grand Rapids, Mich.: Zondervan, 1965.

The Power of Prayer. R.A. Torrey. Grand Rapids, Mich.: Zondervan, 1974.

The Prayer Life. Andrew Murray. Chicago, Ill.: Moody Press, n.d.

The Secret of Positive Praying. John Bisagno. Grand Rapids, Mich.: Zondervan, 1986.

Too Busy Not to Pray. Bill Hybles. Downers Grove, Ill.: Inter-Varsity Press, 1986. How to slow down and spend time with God.

Transforming Your Prayer Life: A 7-week Strategy to a More Meaningful Relationship with God. Dr. Bob Beltz, copyright. Brentwood, Tenn.: Wolgemuth & Hyatt, 1991.

What Happens when Women Pray. Evelyn Christenson and Viola Blake. Wheaton, Ill.: Victor Books, 1976.

When You Pray. Harold Lindsell. Grand Rapids, Mich.: Baker Book House, 1957.

With One Accord. Armin R. Gesswein. Harrisburg, Pa.: Christian Publications, Inc., 1978.

Why Pray? B. J. Wilhite. Lake Mary, Fla.: Creation House, 1988.

Drawing Closer To God

Conversation with God: Experience Intimacy with God through Personal Prayer. Lloyd John Ogilvie. Eugene, Ore.: Harvest House Publishers, 1993. Learning to listen to God as well as speak. Has a thirty-day guide to help make conversation with God a part of your daily life.

Daring to Draw Near. John White. Downers Grove, Ill.: Inter-Varsity Press, 1977. Ten Biblical people and their prayers used to give examples of prayer principles.

Experiencing God: Knowing and Doing the Will of God. Henry Blackaby and Claude V. King. Nashville, Tenn.: LifeWay Press, 1990. A workbook to point persons toward a love relationship with God.

Hearing God. Peter Lord. Grand Rapids, Mich.: Baker Book House, 1988. Learning to distinguish God's voice from all others and avoiding pitfalls. Easy to follow, step-by-step guide to two-way communication with God.

How to Keep a Spiritual Journal. Ronald Klug. Nashville, Tenn.: Thomas Nelson, 1982.

How to Listen to God. Charles Stanley. Nashville, Tenn.: Oliver Nelson Books, 1985. Biblical guidelines for distinguishing God's voice from any other voice, showing how God communicates and the way we should listen and act on His words.

Intimate Friendship with God. Joy Dawson. Old Tappan, N.J.: Revell, 1986. Biblical condition for intimate friendship with God and how to pursue it.

Near to the Heart of God. Deborah Kern. Eugene, Ore.: Harvest House Publishers, 1993. Helpful insights into and suggestions for intimacy with God for those already seeking such a relationship.

No Easy Road. Dick Eastman. Grand Rapids, Mich.: Baker Book House, 1965. A classic, stirring guidebook to understanding the components of successful prayer. *Journey of Power* is a thirteen-lesson course with teacher/student manuals, audio tapes, and study guide based on this book. Contact Dick Eastman (See "Prayer in the Church" for address.)

Practice of the Presence of God. Brother Lawrence. Old Tappan, N.J.: Revell, 1956. A classic.

Prayer: Conversing with God. Rosalind Rinker. Grand Rapids, Mich.: Zondervan, 1959. A classic on an effective method of increasing the joy and meaning of your prayers.

The God Who Hears. W. Bingham Hunter. Downers Grove, Ill.: Inter-Varsity Press, 1986. Getting to know God more intimately through understanding who He is. Answers many important questions about God and the process of prayer.

The Hour that Changes the World. Dick Eastman. Grand Rapids, Mich.: Baker Book House, 1978. Divides a prayer hour into twelve ten-minute segments to give balance and full coverage to your prayer time. *Practical Prayer Life* is a thirteen-lesson course based on this book. Adult and youth editions with transparencies, instructor manual. (See "Prayer in the Church" for address.)

The Knowledge of the Holy. A.W. Tozer. New York, N.Y.: Harper and Row, 1975. A classic.

Intercession   *A Call to Prayer: Intercession in Action.* Germaine Copeland. Explores many aspects and types of intercession and gives guidelines.

Love on Its Knees. Dick Eastman. Old Tappan, N.J.: Chosen Books, 1989. Principles of intercession to help you pray with dramatic effectiveness for unknown people in foreign lands, as well as for your own loved ones.

The Ministry of Intercession. F. J. Huegel. Minneapolis, Minn.: Bethany Fellowship, 1967. A short but powerful book describing how intercession works and how and when to use it.

Prayer Is Invading the Impossible. Jack W. Hayford. Plainfield, N.J.: Logos International, 1977. A "how to" book on strengthening inner faith needed for prayer.

World Prayer Map. Available from Every Home for Christ (World Literature Crusade) 7899 Lexington, Colorado Springs, CO 80920; (719) 260-8888. Excellent full-color map showing each country's population, the current national leader, percent of Christians, amount of access, etc. Has a thirty-one-day prayer strategy to pray for each country and various ministries in these nations.

Destined for the Throne. Paul E. Billheimer. Fort Washington, Pa.: Christian Literature Crusade, 1975

How I Know God Answers Prayer. Rosalind Goforth. Chicago, Ill.: Moody Press, n.d.

Principles for Effective Intercession. Joy Dawson. Youth with a Mission, P.O. Box 296, Sunland, CA 91040.

What Happens When We Pray for Our Families. Evelyn Christenson. Wheaton, Ill.: Victor Books, 1992.

A Celebration of Praise. Dick Eastman. Grand Rapids, Mich.: Baker Book House, 1984. Surveys different facets of God's person in order to have praise the true depth of His nature. Forty-nine praise words given with suggestions for weekly praise and meditation.

The Hallelujah Factor. Jack Taylor. Nashville, Tenn.: Broadman Press, 1983.

The Ultimate Priority. John McArthur. Chicago, Ill.: Moody Press, 1983.

Worship His Majesty. Jack W. Hayford. Waco, Tex.: Word Publishers 1987. A classic book on worship, emphasizing the focus of worship being on God and the power worship has to change people. Worship is foundational to God's blessings on lives. Through it there is brought about an infusion of God's presence which flows into the setting of worship.

Praise/Worship/ Thanksgiving

Revival: The Rain from Heaven. Arthur Wallis. Old Tappan, N.J.: Fleming H. Revell Co., 1979. Helps understand the nature and purpose of revival, and learn how to prepare for it, expect it, and experience its results.

Campus Aflame. J. Edwin Orr. Glendale, Calif.: Regal Books Division, G/L Publications, 1971.

Revival. Richard Owen Roberts. Wheaton, Ill.: Tyndale House Publishers, 1982.

State of the Church. Andrew Murray. Fort Washington, Pa: Christian Literature Crusade, 1983.

The Flaming Tongue. J. Edwin Orr. Chicago, Ill.: Moody Press, 1975.

God's Laws of Revival. Armin Gesswein. Revival Prayer Fellowship, 26076 "C" Getty, Laguna Niguel, CA 92677.

Revival

George Muller: Man of Faith and Miracles. Basil Miller. Minneapolis, Minn.: Zondervan, 1941. A remarkable story of a man of great faith and prayer who ran an orphanage in England.

Praying Hyde. Francis McGraw. Chicago, Ill.: Moody Press, n.d. An ordinary missionary to India becomes extraordinary through prayer.

Rees Howells: Intercessor. Norman P. Grubb. Fort Washington, Pa.: Christian Literature Crusade, 1962. Principles of prevailing prayer help Grubb become the channel of a mighty revival in Africa.

Answers to Prayer. George Mueller. Chicago, Ill.: Moody Press, n.d.

Biography of Praying People

| Fasting | *The Adventure of Fasting.* James Lee Beall. Old Tappan N.J.: Fleming H. Revell Co., 1974. Practical guidebook on fasting, answering many questions concerning fasting. |

God's Chosen Fast. Arthur Wallis. Fort Washington, Pa.: Christian Literature Crusade, 1968. A handbook dealing with all the main fasting passages in Scripture and the practical issues involved.

Fasting: A Neglected Discipline. David Rushworth Smith. Chichester, England: New Wine Press, 1988.

| Prayer for Evangelization, Missions, and the World | *Operation World. Patrick Johnstone.* (5th edition) Pasadena, Calif.: William Carey Library, 1993. Excellent handbook for all countries of the world giving religious, political, economic, etc. information, and prayer requests. Good section on 10/40 window. |

Touch the World Through Prayer. Wesley L. Duewel. Grand Rapids, Mich.: Zondervan, 1986. A powerful handbook on the effectiveness of prayer for evangelism and how to use it in your life.

Unleashing the Power of Prayer. Edited and compiled by Vonette Bright and Ben Jennings. Chicago, Ill.: Moody Press, 1989. Thirty messages from top Christian leader's around the world on personal prayer and world evangelization given to the 1984 International Prayer Assembly for World Evangelization in Seoul, Korea.

With Concerts of Prayer. David Bryant. Ventura, Calif.: Gospel Light Inc./Regal Books, 1984. A classic handbook on explaining what concerts of prayer are, how to hold them in various settings, and how to unite for spiritual revival through prayer It has a small group study guide as part of the book.

| Prayer in the Church | *Churches that Pray.* C. Peter Wagner. Ventura, Calif.: Regal Books, 1993. |

Helping the Church Become a House of Prayer. Leon Franck. Copyright pending. Can be obtained through Prayer Valley, R. 2, Welsh Coulee Rd, La Crosse, WI 54601. $10. Addresses issues for a church wanting to establish a ministry of prayer, appoint a prayer director, or have a prayer room. Also gives ideas to improve the mid-week prayer meeting, corporate and private prayer.

Houses of Prayer. Renewal International. P.O. Box 27994, Concord, CA 94527-0994, (510) 685-4846. How to organize evangelistic prayer groups for neighborhoods.

The Praying Church Sourcebook. Alvin J. Vander Griend. 1990 Church Development Resources, 2850 Kalamazoo Ave. SE, Grand Rapids, MI 49560. $49.50. An excellent 270-page loose-leaf resource notebook for any praying church. Includes such topics as Keys to a Praying; Strategies for Praying Churches including material on the prayer coordinator, different types of prayer groups, the set up and running of the prayer room, and prayer retreats; Stories of Praying Christians; and Resources for Praying Churches. Also an exhaustive list of books, agencies, programs, films, tapes, newsletters, and people who can help churches and individuals develop a life of prayer. Rights of reproduction granted to church making purchase.

Prayer Bulletin Insert. Church Development Resources. 2850 Kalamazoo Ave. SE, Grand Rapids, MI 49560. 50 copies $3, bimonthly. (Free samples upon request.) Includes stories of answered prayer, ideas for prayer ministries, brief teaching articles on prayer, and information on prayer resources.

The Pastor's Prayer Partners. John Maxwell. Bonita, Calif.: Injoy Ministries, 1989. Dr. Maxwell has one of the most effective prayer partners ministry in the country and shares the how to's of starting one. Includes audio tapes.

How to Have a Prayer Ministry. C. Peter Wagner. Pasadena, Calif.: Charles E. Fuller Institute, 1990. A self-study kit with notebook, video and six audio cassettes providing teaching on the contemporary prayer movement, renewal, personal growth and power in ministry.

In His Presence. Prayerworks. A prayer seminar focusing on the A.C.T.S. formula. 38-00 Arrowhead Springs, San Bernardino, CA 92414.

The Doctrine of Prayer. T.W. Hunt. Nashville, Tenn.: Convention Press, 1986

Disciple's Prayer Life: Walking in Fellowship with God. T. W. Hunt and Catherine Walker. Nashville, Tenn.: Convention Press, 1988. An excellent intensive study of prayer for the individual or group. Includes a leader's guide.

Making Room to Pray. Terry Teykl. Manual on how to develop a prayer center or prayer room for your church. Renewal Ministries, Inc., 6501 E. Hway 6 Bypass, College Station, TX 77845.

Hedging in the Pastor Prayer Guide. Terry Teykl. Specific prayer steps to pray protection for your pastor. (See above for address.)

The Southern Baptists have developed many excellent prayer tools which can help a church. Contact them at 127 9th Ave. N., Nashville, TN 37234. Ask for materials by T.W. Hunt, Avery Willis, and Henry Blackaby.

Various materials on prayer for the church are available from Dick Eastman, World Literature Crusade (formerly Change the World Ministries), 7899 Lexington Dr., Colorado Springs, CO 80920; (719) 260-8888

Prayerworks. Earl Pickard. Available for on-site awakening, equipping, and mobilizing of prayer in local churches and communities. Also, Citizens Who Care. Materials available to help you set up prayer coverage for public officials. Contact Prayerworks, P.O. Box 12301, Wichita, KS 67277; (316) 729-0685.

Prayer Resources, INC. Exists to help believers and churches be disciplined and equipped in prayer and make it a priority. 5995 Mingle Dr., Memphis, TN 32115.

Possessing the Gates of the Enemy. Cindy Jacobs. Tarrytown, N.Y.: Chosen Books, 1991. In depth intercession strategies as well as common pitfalls to avoid in prayer.   Spiritual Warfare

Prayer Shield. C. Peter Wagner. Ventura, Calif.: Regal Books, 1992. How to intercede for pastors, Christian leaders and others on the spiritual front lines.

Prayerwalking. Steve Hawthorne and Graham Kendrick. Lake Mary, Fla.: Creation House, 1992. How to pray on-site with insight. A practical menu of biblically based, proven ideas to begin preparing whole cities for spiritual awakening by praying for your community.

Taking Our Cities for God. John Dawson. Lake Mary, Fla.: Creation House, 1989. Handbook on identifying and breaking through prayer spiritual strongholds in your city so evangelism and discipleship can be more effective.

The Believer's Guide to Spiritual Warfare. Thomas B. White. Ann Arbor, Mich.: Servant Publications, 1990.

The Handbook for Spiritual Warfare. Dr. Ed Murphy. Nashville, Tenn.: Thomas Nelson, 1992. A Biblically based in-depth look at all sides of the subject by this Bible professor.

The Mighty Warrior. Elizabeth Alves. Bulverde, Tex.: Canopy Press, 1992. An excellent handbook covering such topics as the purpose of prayer, types, hearing from God, spiritual warfare, and weapons of warfare.

The Spiritual Warrior's Prayer Guide. Quin Sherren & Ruthanne Garlock. Ann Arbor, Mich.: Servant Publications, 1992. Teaches you how to use the Scriptures to stop enemy attacks in all areas of life. Many practical Scriptures are given on various topics of daily living.

Warfare Prayer. C. Peter Wagner. Ventura, Calif.: Regal Books, 1992. How to seek God's power and protection in the battle to build His Kingdom.

Videos, 16mm Films, Audio Tapes

Ten-Minute Messages. J. O. Sanders.
Tape # 201:
1. Hindrances to Prayer 9:03
2. Praying in Jesus' Name 9:54
3. Praying According to the Will of God 10:12
4. Turning the Promises of Prayer into Fact 10:33
5. The Prayer of Faith 10:29
6. Praying with Authority 10:30

Tape # 202
1. The Intercessory Work of Moses, Aaron, and Hur 9:30
2. The Power of United Prayer 10:38
3. Praying Without Ceasing 9:56
4. The Prayer of Paul 10:20
5. The Ministry of Intercession 10:12
6. Prayer for World Rulers 9:46
Tapes are $2.00 each and are available through Overseas Missionary Fellowship, 10 W. Dry Creek Cir. Littleton, CO 80120; (303) 730-4160, (800) 422-5330, and Fax (303) 730-4165

The Role of Prayer in Spiritual Awakening. Dr. J. Edwin Orr. Twenty-six-minute presentation on prayer and its impact on society in times of revival. Highly motivational. Rental of video and 16mm is through Prayerworks, (909) 886-5224, ext. 5575. For sale in video format from Key Note Communications, 1-800-352-8273.

How You Can Pray with Confidence. Dr. Bill Bright. Booklet, video (about thirty minutes), audio tape available from Key Note Communications, 1-800-352-8273.

How to Have a Prayer Ministry. C. Peter Wagner. (See entry under "Prayer in the Church.")

Various audio tapes and some video tapes are available from the following ministries. You may contact them for information and catalogues:

David Bryant Concerts of Prayer Int., Pentagon Towers, P.O. Box 36008, Minneapolis, MN 55435.

Evelyn Christenson United Prayer Ministries, 4265 Brigadoon Dr., St. Paul, MN 55126; (612) 566-5390.

Joy Dawson Youth with a Mission, Box 591, Tujunga, CA 91042; (818) 352-3070.

Dick Eastman World Literature Crusade (Every Home for Christ), 7899 Lexington Dr., Colorado Springs, CO 80920 (719) 260-8888.

Pastor Jack Hayford, Living Way Ministries, 14300 Sherman Way, Van Nuys, CA 91405; (818) 779-8180.

Pastor David Jeremiah, Turning Point Ministries, 1-800-947-1993.

Pastor John McArthur Grace to You Ministries 1-800 554-7223.

Glenn Sheppard International Prayer Ministries, 3322 Irving Bridge Rd., Conyers, GA 30207; (404) 388-7616.

Pastor Charles Stanley, In Touch Ministries 1-800-323-3747.

Newsletters and Prayer Magazines

Global Prayer Digest, U.S. Center for World Mission, 1605 E. Elizabeth Str., Pasadena, CA 91104.

Intercessors for America Newsletter, P.O. Box 2639, Reston, VA 22091.

National Prayer Leaders Newsletter, P.O. Box 36008, Minneapolis, MN 55435.

National Prayer Movement Forum and *Prayer Net,* Concerts of Prayer Int. P.O. Box 7383, Madison, WI 53707.

Prayer Bulletin Insert, Church Development Resources, 2850 Kalamazoo Ave. SE, Grand Rapids, MI 49560.

International Intercessors, P.O. Box O, Pasadena, CA 91109.

Forgiveness
and Difficult People

God expects you to live at peace with all people to the best of your ability (Rom. 12:18). With some, this is easy, but there are always those few (or many) who seem to irritate you, even threaten you when you are around them. They may have done terrible things to you, hurting you emotionally if not physically. This can especially be true of parents and siblings.* How can we live at peace with such people? God provides the answer.

This will mean forgiving *carte blanche* what they have done, no matter how offensive and inhumane it may seem—not because the person deserves or has earned your forgiveness, but because you are obeying the Lord's command of Ephesians 4:32. You may need to pray a prayer like this:

Father, I come to You with all the hurt I feel toward _____. You know how much I have been wounded by what he/she has done. In my own flesh and strength I can not forgive him/her. But I know You want me to, and so I choose to forgive him/her by an act of my will in obedience to You and not based on my feelings. Heal my emotions and help my feelings come into alignment with what I have chosen to do now. Let me not only feel forgiveness for _____, but let me also start to see him/her as You see him/her. Let me care about him/her as You love him/her.

Then, every time you have a negative thought toward this person, or are reminded of a bad experience with him/her, simply say, "Thank You, Lord, that for helping me to forgive _____for that and to see him/her as You see him/her." You may also want to try praying something positive for the person at that time to counteract the temptation to dwell on the negative.

Are you being "I centered" by wanting your rights, revenge, justice, or fairness? Remember, the Lord says that vengeance is His and He will repay (Rom. 12:19) and that believers are to be "dead men."

Things to remember and do when dealing with difficult people:

- God created them and loves them. Ask God to show you them as He sees them. Try to have His heart for the individuals.

- You need to want to forgive and interact with them kindly because of your love for the Lord.

- Our enemy is the accuser of the brethren (Rev. 12:10). Therefore, he will make sure you notice every negative thing someone does. He will also try to make you suspicious of their motives and actions. When you "buy" what he is selling, then you are doing his will, not God's. So choose not to cooperate with him.

- Pray positive scriptural truths into the persons' lives, but pray them for yourself first so they do not become a club in your hand.

See resource 16K for a sample prayer on praying Scripture for a difficult person.

---

* A person's view of God can be adversely affected by a human father's negative impact on his/her life. Therefore it is very important that a person purposely forgives the parent in order to have a clear understanding of God.

Sample
Sermon Outlines

Knowing God Through Prayer

Introduction:

1. Open your Bibles to Matthew 6. Today I want to begin a new series titled "Prayer Can Make a Difference."
2. Definition of prayer: talking to God.
3. Why would God want to hear? Why would He even listen?
4. Matthew 6:9, "This . . . is how you should pray: 'Our Father in heaven, hallowed be your name.'"
5. Why is God interested? Because He is the perfect "Father in heaven."
6. What kind of father?

   I. He is the Father who never hurts.

      A. Psalm 103:13: "As a father has compassion on his children, so the Lord has compassion on those who fear him."

      B. He cares in a perfect way.

      C. 1 Peter 5:7: "Cast all your anxiety on him because he cares for you."

   II. He is the Father who never changes.

      A. James 1:17: "Every good and perfect gift is from above, coming down from the Father of the heavenly lights, who does not change like shifting shadows."

      B. 2 Timothy 2:13: "If we are faithless, he will remain faithful, for he cannot disown himself."

      C. God never has a bad day.

   III. He is the Father who never leaves.

      A. Acts 17:27: "God did this so that men would seek him and perhaps reach out for him and find him, though he is not far from each one of us."

      B. He's never too busy for me.

C. Psalm 145:18: "The Lord is near to all who call on him, to all who call on him in truth."

D. When you're feeling low, He's there with you.

E. Psalm 34:18: "The Lord is close to the broken-hearted and saves those who are crushed in spirit."

IV. He is the Father who never fails.

A. Human fathers will fail; God doesn't.

B. Luke 1:37: "'For nothing is impossible with God.'"

C. Ephesians 3:20 "Now to him who is able to do immeasurably more than all we ask or imagine, according to his power that is at work within us")

Conclusion

1. As our heavenly Father, God always takes care of His children.

2. Are you a child of God?

God Can Meet Your Needs

Introduction

1. Matthew 6:9: "'Hallowed be your name.'"

2. Names are a big deal. Back in the Old Testament times, names were a big deal too.

3. In fact, a name represented your character.

4. Let's look at four names of God that help us to see God's character and comprehend His ability to meet our needs.

I. God is our Provider.

A. Jehovah-Jireh, Genesis 22:14: "So Abraham called that place The Lord Will Provide. And to this day it is said, 'On the mountain of the Lord it will be provided.'"

B. Share the story of Abraham and Isaac.

C. What needs will God provide? 2 Peter 1:3: "His divine power has given us everything we need for life and godliness through our knowledge of him who called us by his own glory and goodness."

II. God is our righteousness.

A. Jehovah-Tsidkenu; Jeremiah 23:6: "In his days Judah will be saved and Israel will live in safety. This is the name by which he will be called: The Lord Our Righteousness."

B. He removes my guilt and forgives my faults.

C. Isaiah 43:25: "'I, even I, am he who blots out your transgressions, for my own sake, and remembers your sins no more.'"

D. We need to confess, 1 John 1:9: "If we confess our sins, he is faithful and just and will forgive us our sins and purify us from all unrighteousness."

III. God is our peace.

A. Jehovah-Shalom; Judges 6:24: "So Gideon built an altar to the Lord there and called it The Lord is Peace. To this day it stands in Ophrah of the Abiezrites."
B. Share story of Gideon.
C. Whatever your stress, God can bring you peace.
IV. God is our Healer.
A. Jehovah-Rophe; Exodus 15:26: "He said, 'If you listen carefully to the voice of the Lord your God and do what is right in his eyes, if you pay attention to his commands and keep all his decrees, I will not bring on you any of the diseases I brought on the Egyptians, for I am the LORD who heals you.'")
B. Physical, mental, emotional and spiritual hurts
C. Psalm 147:3 "He heals the brokenhearted and binds up their wounds."
Conclusion
1. Greatest name for God? Philippians 2:9–11: "Therefore God exalted him to the highest place and gave him the name that is above every name, that at the name of Jesus every knee should bow, in heaven and on earth and under the earth, and every tongue confess that Jesus Christ is Lord, to the glory of God the Father."
2. Jehovah of the Old Testament is the Jesus of the New Testament.
3. Jesus Christ alone can meet those needs.

There's a Reason to Live
Introduction
1. Open to Matthew 6 to continue our series on prayer.
2. Let me ask you a question: Why are you alive? What's the reason for living?
3. Matthew 6:10: "'Your kingdom come, your will be done on earth as it is in heaven.'"
4. There are four reasons for your life.
   I. You are here to know God.
   A. Ephesians 1:4–5: "For he chose us in him before the creation of the world to be holy and blameless in his sight. In love he predestined us to be adopted as his sons through Jesus Christ, in accordance with his pleasure and will."
   B. God has no illegitimate children; we all have purpose.
   C. The more we know God, the more we love Him.
   II. You are here to become Christlike.
   A. Romans 8:28–29: "And we know that in all things God works for the good of those who love him, who have been called according to his purpose. For those God foreknew he also predestined to be conformed to

the likeness of his Son, that he might be the first born among many brothers."

B. Unlike other creation, we were made in God's image.

C. All that happens is God molding us into that image.

III. You are here to serve God.

A. God has always had jobs for man to do.

B. Adam, manage the garden; Nehemiah, build a wall; Paul, plant churches.

C. Acts 13:36: "'For when David had served God's purpose in his own generation.'"

D. Romans 12:1–2: "Therefore, I urge you, brothers, in view of God's mercy, to offer your bodies as living sacrifices, holy and pleasing to God—this is your spiritual act of worship."

IV. You are here to get ready to live with God.

A. 2 Corinthians 5:1, 5: "Now we know that if the earthly tent we live in is destroyed, we have a building from God, an eternal house in heaven, not built by human hands…Now it is God who has made us for this very purpose and has given us the Spirit as a deposit, guaranteeing what is to come."

B. All God's children will one day be in heaven.

C. Earth is a temporary training ground.

Conclusion

1. How do you get to heaven? Become a Christian and seek His kingdom.

2. John 6:40: "'For my Father's will is that everyone who looks to the Son and believes in him shall have eternal life, and I will raise him up at the last day.'"

3. Matthew 6:33: "But seek first his kingdom and his righteousness, and all these things will be given to you as well."

The Forgiveness of God

Introduction

1. We're doing a series on the Lord's Prayer, and we have come to "'Forgive us our debts.'"

2. Romans 3:23 tells us that we all have sinned.

3. So, if we are guilty before a holy God, how can we get forgiveness in our lives? Simple. Ask for it.

4. And God will forgive you in three ways.

I. God will forgive you instantly.

A. Nehemiah 9:17: "They refused to listen and failed to remember the miracles you performed among them. They became stiff-necked and in their rebellion appointed a leader in order to return to their slavery. But you are a forgiving God, gracious and compassionate, slow to anger and abounding in love. Therefore you did not desert them."

B. God is waiting to forgive you. Why wait to ask?

C. Isaiah 55:7: "Let the wicked forsake his way and the evil man his thoughts. Let him turn to the LORD, and he will have mercy on him, and to our God, for he will freely pardon."

II. God will forgive you totally.

A. Colossians 2:13–14: "When you were dead in your sins and in the uncircumcision of your sinful nature, God made you alive with Christ. He forgave us all our sins, having canceled the written code, with its regulations, that was against us and that stood opposed to us; he took it away, nailing it to the cross."

B. He never holds back, and He never holds a grudge.

C. God's forgiveness is complete.

III. God will forgive you frequently.

A. 1 John 1:9: "If we confess our sins, he is faithful and just and will forgive us our sins and purify us from all unrighteousness."

B. Romans 3:23–24: "For all have sinned and fall short of the glory of God, and are justified freely by his grace through the redemption that came by Christ Jesus."

C. Have you ever committed the same sin? God was not shocked and is willing to forgive.

Conclusion

1. Romans 8:1: "Therefore, there is now no condemnation for those who are in Christ Jesus."

2. Asking for forgiveness from God is as easy as A-B-C.

A—Admit your sin.

B—Believe in Christ's power to forgive.

C—Commit your life to Jesus.

Praying Your Way Through Worry

Introduction

1. Matthew 6:11: "'Give us today our daily bread.'"

2. Are you a worrier? In this one verse, God reminds us of three keys for overcoming worry through prayer.

I. Ask for God's help.

A. "*Give us* today our daily bread" (emphasis added).

B. James 4:2: "You want something but don't get it. You kill and covet, but you cannot have what you want. You quarrel and fight. You do not have, because you do not ask God."

C. Twenty times in the New Testament we are told to ask.

II. Recognize God's resources.

A. "Give us today our daily *bread*." (emphasis added). Bread was a staple needed in the Jewish home.

B. Philippians 4:19: "And my God will meet all your needs according to his glorious riches in Christ Jesus."

C. Romans 8:32: "He who did not spare his own Son, but gave him up for us all—how will he not also, along with him, graciously give us all things?"

III. Trust God's timing

A. "Give us *today* our *daily* bread" (emphasis added).

B. God's timing may not be yours, but trust Him. His timing is perfect.

C. Daily bread, not weekly, monthly, or annually.

D. Must have faith.

E. Romans 10:17: "Consequently, faith comes from hearing the message, and the message is heard through the word of Christ."

F. Psalm 68:19: "Praise be to the Lord, to God our Savior, who daily bears our burdens."

Conclusion: what will happen if I pray through these three trusts? three things . . .

A. I will be at peace.

B. I will have an eternal perspective.

C. I will sense God's purpose.

Praying Through Temptation

Introduction

1. Matthew 6:13: "'And lead us not into temptation, but deliver us from the evil one.'"

2. God doesn't expect you to be perfect, but God has made it possible for you to sin less. How? P-R-A-Y.

I. P—Pray for strength.

A. Ephesians 6:10–11: "Finally, be strong in the Lord and in his mighty power. Put on the full armor of God so that you can take your stand against the devil's schemes."

B. Satan's #1 strategy is to get you afraid.

C. Hebrews 4:15: "For we do not have a high priest who is unable to sympathize with our weaknesses, but we have one who has been tempted in every way, just as we are—yet was without sin."

II. R—Request help from God.

A. Psalms 50:15: "'And call upon me in the day of trouble; I will deliver you, and you will honor me.'"

B. Have you ever been tempted to steal? Cheat? Lie?

C. Call on the Lord at those difficult times.

III. A—Ask for a new focus.

A. There are three stages to a temptation: attention, arousal, action.

B. Pray for a refocusing of your thoughts and desires before the last two.

C. James 1:14–15: "But each one is tempted when, by his own evil desires, he is dragged away and enticed. Then, after desire has conceived, it gives birth to sin; and sin, when it is full-grown, gives birth to death."

D. Proverbs 4:23: "Above all else, guard your affections. For they influence everything else in your life" (TLB).

IV. Y—Yield to a friend.

A. Ecclesiastes 4:9–10: "Two are better than one, because they have a good return for their work: If one falls down, his friend can help him up. But pity the man who falls and has no one to help him up!"

B. James 5:16: "Therefore confess your sins to each other and pray for each other so that you may be healed. The prayer of a righteous man is powerful and effective."

C. We all need a special someone for accountability and help.

Conclusion

1. 1 Corinthians 10:13: "No temptation has seized you except what is common to man. And God is faithful; he will not let you be tempted beyond what you can bear. But when you are tempted, he will also provide a way out so that you can stand up under it."

2. Two truths:

A. Temptation is common.

B. Common temptations have a common solution.

3. You will never be sinless on earth, but through prayers you can sin less.

Evaluating
Your Spiritual Life

In spending time with the Lord, a spiritual inventory is extremely helpful. God teaches to come before Him with clean hearts, souls, and minds. As you go forth to do battle, you must have a pure heart before Him. God promises that, "If my people, who are called by my name, will humble themselves and pray and seek my face and turn from their wicked ways, then will I hear from heaven and will forgive their sin and will heal their land" (2 Chron. 7:14).

Search me, O God, and know my heart; test me and know my anxious thoughts. See if there is any offensive way in me, and lead me in the way everlasting (Ps. 139:23–24).

He who conceals his sins does not prosper, but whoever confesses and renounces them finds mercy (Prov. 28:13).

If I had cherished sin in my heart, the Lord would not have listened (Ps. 66:18).

Begin your inventory with a simple prayer:

Father, You know my weakness in the area of _____. I've not been able to conquer this, even though I've tried. I know this is not pleasing to You and grieves Your heart. I give you permission to reveal the things I need to work on and permission for you to change me.

Walk with the Lord

As the deer pants for streams of water, so my soul pants for you, O God. My soul thirsts for God, for the living God. When can I go and meet with God?" (Ps. 42:1–2)

O God, you are my God, earnestly I seek you; my soul thirsts for you, my body longs for you, in a dry and weary land where there is no water (Ps. 63:1).

Questions   1. Are you satisfied with how your heart longs for God?
2. Do you look forward to seeking Him and having fellowship with Him?
3. Are your prayer times "high points" in your day?

Relationships

Roommates, family, fellow workers, friends, and neighbors.

Love is patient, love is kind. It does not envy, it does not boast, it is not proud. It is not rude, it is not self-seeking, it is not easily angered, it keeps no record of wrongs. Love does not delight in evil but rejoices with the truth (1 Cor. 13:4–6).

"A new command I give you: Love one another. As I have loved you, so you must love one another" (John 13:34).

Questions   1. Would you say you have God's *agape* love for others?
2. Are you known as a kind person?
3. Do you remember the wrongs people do to you?

Then make my joy complete by being like-minded, having the same love, being one in spirit and purpose. Do nothing out of selfish ambition or vain conceit, but in humility consider others better than yourselves. Each of you should look not only to your own interests, but also to the interests of others (Phil. 2:2–4).

Pride only breeds quarrels (Prov. 13:10).

A man's pride brings him low (Prov. 29:23).

Questions   1. How often do you "consider others better than yourself"?
2. Do you ever entertain the thought that others are lucky to have you as a friend?
3. How much do you think about the needs of others?
4. When was the last time you shared with those closest to you how much you appreciate them?

Be kind and compassionate to one another, forgiving each other, just as in Christ God forgave you (Eph. 4:32).

Therefore, as God's chosen people, holy and dearly loved, clothe yourselves with compassion, kindness, humility, gentleness and patience. Bear with each other and forgive whatever grievances you may have against one another. Forgive as the Lord forgave you. And over all these virtues put on love, which binds them all together in perfect unity. Let the peace of Christ rule in your hearts, since as members of one body you were called to peace. And be thankful (Col. 3:12-15).

Bless those who persecute you; bless and do not curse...Live in harmony with one another. Do not be proud, but be willing to associate with people of low position. Do not be conceited. Do not repay anyone evil for evil. Be careful to do what is right in the eyes of everybody. If it is possible, as far as it depends on you, live at peace with everyone (Rom. 12:14, 16–18).

Questions

1. Is there someone the Holy Spirit brings to mind you need to forgive? Recently or from the past?
2. Is there someone that every time you think of them you are pained because of memories of what they've done?
3. Do you find it difficult to have compassion for those who fall short of your expectations?

Let your conversation be always full of grace, seasoned with salt, so that you may know how to answer everyone (Col. 4:6).

He who guards his lips guards his soul, but he who speaks rashly will come to ruin (Prov. 13:3).

Through patience a ruler can be persuaded, and a gentle tongue can break a bone (Prov. 25:15).

Do not let any unwholesome talk come out of your mouths, but only what is helpful for building others up according to their needs, that it may benefit those who listen. And do not grieve the Holy Spirit of God, with whom you were sealed for the day of redemption. Get rid of all bitterness, rage and anger, brawling and slander, along with every form of malice (Eph. 4:29–31).

Do not lie to each other (Col. 3:9).

Questions

1. Do you think before speaking?
2. Do you try to say kind things, even to the difficult people in your life?
3. Do you find yourself talking about other people in an unloving way and only when they're not present?
4. Are you open to listening to others about the problems they're having with another person for the purpose of just "knowing," not helping.
5. Do you like to tease people about their weaknesses, mannerisms, peculiarities, eating habits, or fears?

6. Are you always careful to tell the truth?

Thought Life/Self Control

Finances, health, temptations, difficulties, and attitude toward work)

> Put to death, therefore, whatever belongs to your earthly nature: sexual immorality, impurity, lust, evil desires and greed, which is idolatry (Col. 3:5).

> Like a city whose walls are broken down is a man who lacks self-control (Prov. 25:28).

Questions
1. Do you struggle with impure thoughts and temptations that you give into?
2. Do you find yourself thinking about doing things you know or suspect are not pleasing to God?
3. Do you ever find yourself "out of control" or doing things you later wish you hadn't?

> For God did not give us a spirit of timidity, but a spirit of power, of love and of self-discipline (2 Tim. 1:7).

Questions
1. Do you worry about your safety or that of your family?
2. Are your finances a continual distraction?
3. How are your social contacts and relationships causing you stress?

> One who is slack in his work is brother to one who destroys (Prov. 18:9).

> Turn my eyes away from worthless things; preserve my life according to your word (Ps. 119:37).

> I will set before my eyes no vile thing. The deeds of faithless men I hate; they will not cling to me (Ps. 101:3).

Questions
1. Do you watch or read questionable things?
2. Do you go to movies that you'd be uncomfortable with some people knowing you'd seen?

The Biblical Solution

> Cast all your anxiety on him because he cares for you. Be self-controlled and alert. Your enemy the devil prowls around like a roaring lion looking for someone to devour (1 Pet. 5:7–8).

> Submit yourselves, then, to God. Resist the devil, and he will flee from you (Jas. 4:7).

> Set your minds on things above, not on earthly things (Col. 3:2).

Finally, brothers, whatever is true, whatever is noble, whatever is right, whatever is pure, whatever is lovely, whatever is admirable—if anything is excellent or praiseworthy—think about such things (Phil. 4:8).

Trust in the LORD with all your heart and lean not on your own understanding; in all your ways acknowledge him, and he will make your paths straight (Prov. 3:5–6).

Let another praise you, and not your own mouth; someone else, and not your own lips (Prov. 27:2).

As you consider the need for revival, you should look at what God has just shown you in the above sections. You may have found areas that have kept you from being completely Spirit controlled. But now you have breathed spiritually and are ready to ask Him for a deeper commitment of your life and closer walk with Him.

The following is a sample prayer you can pray, or you can pray in your own words using these concepts.

Father, thank You for the cleansing You have just done in my life. I long to live a perfect and holy life before You. I know this is what You desire. But, it seems that sometimes I let things crowd You out; that I don't really know how to love and worship You the way I see David and others doing in the Scriptures. Let me be like David who longed for You as the thirsty deer longs for water in the middle of a drought. I want to enjoy You as I would my husband/wife, to love You as my most intimate friend. Give me back a "first love" for You, drawing ever closer to You, being more in tune with Your thoughts, Your way. I desire always to be in the absolute center of Your will, doing only what You want, being Your eyes, ears, arms, legs, and voice.

Help me have a meaningful, quality quiet time with You each day. Wake me up refreshed and wide awake. Teach me each day more about You, Your ways.

Let the Scriptures come more alive for me, and be as sweet as honey to me as they were to David, or as to Job who called them more important than his very food. Help me to memorize Your Word and teach me how to meditate on it regularly. Show me how to be in prayer throughout my day. Teach me how to pray effectively for those I love. Show me their needs and then give me Scriptures to claim for them. Teach me to pray Your heart. Let my every thought, my every action, always be pleasing to You.

Suggestions For Transparency

When we speak of transparency, terms of having nothing hidden between you and another person usually come to mind—of being open and above board, of communicating what is on your heart and not trying to shade the truth to make yourself look better. To be transparent involves integrity, honesty, and truthfulness.

Transparency before the Lord is very necessary to live a life that has nothing between you and Him. The enemy wants you to mistrust the Lord, to draw back from Him, to question His goodness and therefore withhold from Him both your trust and your desire for intimacy. Complete trust in God is based on believing fully that He wants the very best for you, that He will not do anything to you or ask anything from you that is not in your absolute best interest. Furthermore, it means having confidence in His abilities to meet your every need, and in general having an unshakable faith in His goodness, deep love, commitment to ,and care for you.

Once a person comes to this place of understanding and trust, transparency before the Lord—being 1000 percent open and honest before Him—is not hard. But getting to that place for most means having to resist a lot of enemy bombardment. Thoughts like, *If I admit this, God won't like me.* (God already knows what you are thinking so you won't shock Him by admitting it openly to Him.) *If I let God take over completely in my life, I may not like what He wants to do or will ask of me. If I ask the Lord to reveal my heart to me as He sees it, He may show me something I'm not willing to give up.* Both statements are an attack on God's goodness, love, and care and are an attempt to undermine your trust in Him.

The last statement along with this next one also includes a false need to protect oneself from God's intervention and the desire to have one's self-worth based on behavior rather than who he or she is in Christ. *I already feel insecure enough in what I do know about me. I don't want to have to deal with anything else that is negative. I won't be able to handle it. It will undermine what little self-confidence I already have.*

If you are to live a life that is able to draw closer to God, and to have His power flowing in and through you, there can be nothing between you and Him. This means no unconfessed sin, a desire to live a sinless life, and the determination to take whatever steps are necessary to become transparent and squeaky clean before Him.

The following prayer is suggested in taking such steps.

Father, I want so much to live a life that is pleasing to You, that is squeaky clean. And I know this is what You want, too. Yet at times, I know, I fall so short. It seems so easy to let little things come between myself and You, not to have full integrity, to compromise at times when I allow my flesh to get the upper hand. [Name any known sins/weaknesses.] Help me to see why I do this, to face it straight on. Then give me the way to overcome this and the courage to do so. Make Your ways, Your desires, the overwhelming desires of my heart. Do whatever it takes to bring me to a point of purity and no compromise or rationalization in even the slightest area. Holy Spirit, point out to me any time I am being less than transparent, am considering a compromising action, or in any other way am about to do something that would be wrong, no matter how small a matter it may seem to me. Show me what the right thing is to do, and then give me the courage to do it no matter what the consequences. Remind me at such times that I can fully trust You, that You will not ask me to do anything that I cannot do or that would be harmful to me in the long run. Increase my desire to live a life of absolute integrity before You every minute of my life.

Verses on which to meditate:
Psalms 1; 51; 119 (especially vv. 1–18, 29–38, 44–48, 52–83, 92–106, 111–120, 125–152, 159–176); 101:3; 112:1; 141:3–4; John 15:10,14; Philippians 2:1–7,14; 4:8; and 1 John 5:2–3.

Prayers and Praying

The following different styles or elements of prayer can be used to give more variety in corporate and personal prayer.

Remember the difference between defensive and offensive praying. Pray defensively to come against things which have already happened and need changing. Pray offensively as a more preventative measure and to attack the enemy to take back what he has wrongly been holding.

Adoring the Lord: worshipping God for His attributes, nature, works, the way He makes you feel, etc.

Confession of Sin: agreeing with God that you have committed a sin, naming it specifically, and then expressing the desire, with His help, never to do it again.

Thanksgiving and Appreciation of All the Lord Has and Is Doing: recognizing and thanking God for what He is daily doing for you and for your church; telling Him how much this means to you; what would be true of your life if He did not do these things, etc.

Interceding: praying for the needs of others, both for things they have asked for in prayer and those things you know God wants for them (like salvation, change of attitudes, etc.). Often there will be empathy (feeling as they do) or identifying with the need involved.

Petition: asking for yourself.

Praying the Scriptures: using the Scriptures to stimulate prayer and expanding on the ideas presented; claiming promises as you read them; thanking God for what a specific

Scripture reveals about His nature or actions; confessing sin the Scripture points out, etc.

Prayer Partners: two persons who covenant to pray together regularly for specific things, such as the church, for each other, for social issues, etc. They usually pray once a week together, but may also pray over the phone when they cannot meet or there is an important request that needs immediate prayer. Often the commitment is such that they pray separately daily for specific needs of the other person or things of mutual concern.

Prayer Triplets: much like prayer partners except three are involved. In addition, salvation of friends and family are often a key focus. For example, each person may have a list of three to five people who need salvation. The other two will pray regularly for them. As a person is saved, a new name will be given to replace that name.

Huddles: three to five people praying for a short time, often at church or in a meeting. Churches have several huddles praying just before the main service. This format is also very effective in group prayer times.

Unison Prayer: like the Lord's Prayer, but it can also be done in unison where each person prays about a subject within a group. This can be done either silently or out loud. In Korea unison praying is often seen in church. It is frequently so loud, you cannot hear anyone else near you, if you pray in a small group, but there is a real sense of much fervent prayer being offered.

Conversational: group praying where no individual dominates the prayer time, although there can be a leader. People pray just a short time, similar to a normal conversation. Several will pray for the same subject, often verbally agreeing with previous pray-ers. No one will introduce another area of prayer until it appears the current one has been covered. This is a very popular group style since it is less intimidating for those still learning how to pray out loud. They can pray just a simple sentence like, "Yes, Lord, I agree" or "Lord, make it happen quickly." Even more experienced pray-ers can pray such short statements and find it refreshing and a relaxed yet meaningful atmosphere in which to seek the Lord. Often a greater unity and intimacy and depth occurs in conversational praying than in more traditional, longer prayer segments.

Led by one: A leader has requests or asks for requests, then either prays for them all from the front, assigns someone else to pray for them all, or can ask for volunteers to pray for each one of the requests.

Small Groups: A larger group breaks up into smaller groups of two to six, depending on the leader's instructions. Then each group prays for the requests. When there are many requests and limited time, a variation on this is to divide the groups, assigning each one a section of the requests.

Prayer Vigil: a number of people focusing concentrated prayer for a specific need and usually for a specific time frame. Often used when an important decision is to be made, for an upcoming evangelistic event, a social concern such as an election or a court or legislative decision, or when there is severe illness or a crisis.

Over the Phone: a God-given opportunity to pray at the time a request is given. Elderly people find this a nice way to pray with others and not have to leave their home. Many people, especially those in ministry, like to pray briefly for the other person on the phone before saying good-bye. This method is a very personal and meaningful way of letting others know you really care about them and their needs and making them feel special.

Special Interest Groups: prayer groups such as missionaries, young people and the sick in the church focusing on special interests, Anything that people feel strongly about, including praying for social issues, can draw them together for prayer.

Eight-, Twelve-, or Twenty-four Hour Chain: a chain of pray-ers for a specific length per day. During the specified hours, someone is praying for the church and congregational requests. This praying often takes place at the church but may also take place at home if the church is not a convenient place. Prayer rooms offer a wonderful opportunity for prayer chains.

Emergency Chain: individuals who have agreed to pray for sudden emergencies, often health or accident related. It is designed to get many people praying as quickly as possible for emergencies. Usually there is a key person who calls several others who have five to ten people under them to contact. For example, number one calls number two who calls number three, etc. If number one cannot quickly contact number two, then he or she calls number three (or four, etc. until they get a hold of someone.) Number one then will continue to call those not readily available until they can be reached. It is wise to have number ten call number one to let the person know the chain is complete.

This way, if number ten does not call back in a reasonable time, number one can try to find out where the break is in the chain.

At the Altar: people coming to the front for a time to be alone with the Lord and deal with whatever He has shown during the service, or to have prayer with another praying person either at the front or in a different room.

Prayer Room: a special room set aside in the church where people can come to pray for the church and congregational requests. Such requests are kept in the room along with other appropriate prayer materials. Missionary prayer letters, denominational prayer requests, congregational requests, church activities, and staff are usually a part of the prayer materials. Evangelistic opportunities and praying for the world are also often included. Many churches will have a telephone line exclusively for incoming prayer requests. In such cases, an answering machine is often used to cover those times no one is in the room.

Prayer Covering: a form of intercession mainly focused on an individual by another individual; for example, a member of the congregation praying for specific needs of the pastor on a regular, informed basis. A high degree of commitment is involved.

Adopt-a-Youth: assigning older members one of the youth to pray for. Information about the youth or needs are given. This can be done anonymously or with higher degree of commitment where they meet together periodically for fellowship and prayer or pray together over the phone—an excellent way to bridge the communication gap between generations and to encourage youth.

Concerts of Prayer: a concerted effort usually held within a community and usually open to believers from all backgrounds to unite them in praying for common prayer interests, especially revival, evangelism, intercession, social concerns, and unity. The name reflects the fact that prayer is like an orchestra made up of many differing instruments which, if brought together to play the same music, can produce a beautiful concert.

Prayer Conferences: are focused on training laity by experienced pray-er or outside person.

Prayer Retreats: held so people can get away from the busy-ness of life and spend time with others or alone with the Lord, and/or the pastor or prayer leader can take key people either in leadership or praying away for a time with the Lord and for planning. Often teaching on prayer will be incorporated. A third prayer retreat format is where an outside speaker holds a type of prayer conference.

Prayer Summits: intense, focused times, usually in an isolated place where pastors or an affinity group will come with trained facilitators to seek the face of the Lord; usually one to five days long.

Featured Film

If possible, show J. Edwin Orr's film, "The Role of Prayer in Spiritual Awakening," and ask and do the following questions and actions.

Questions

- What is a key ingredient in revival? (prayer) Why?
- What kinds of positive affects can revival bring in the individual and in society? Give some examples.
- Is revival needed today? Where? Why?
- What changes would you expect to see if America were to have revival or if your city had true revival?
- What part can you or your church play in opening up the way for God to bring revival? What should you do right now? Later? Who should be involved? (*everyone*)
- What new insights did you get today?
- As a result of seeing this film, are there any decisions you have made you would like to share with the group?

Actions

Before. Pray out loud before the start of the film for the Lord to help everyone understand what He has done in the past through revival. Ask that each one catch a vision of what He can and will do through you if you are open to His Spirit to pray for revival. Ask that He will give you His agenda for such prayer both corporately and individually.

After. Pray that:

- There will be a great desire for people to get right with God.

Resource 10

- God will lay a burden on your hearts to intercede regularly for revival.
- Revival will start in your own hearts right away.
- God will show you anything that is hindering His bringing revival in your lives and the life of the church, including disunity among the brethren both within and without your local church.

You can rent this film from Prayerworks, 38-00 Arrowhead Springs, San Bernardino, Ca 92414; (909) 886-5224 Ext 5575 or fax 909-881-7705.

16mm (26 minutes); rental = $25 per showing;
video = $7.50 per showing
Video can be purchased for $19.95 plus shipping and handling.

Prayer Targets
For the Church

Schools: Teachers, administration, school board, custodial, security, and gang activity; Teach well, no new age materials, good moral values and modeled and communicated, and good student-teacher relationships.

Deut. 4:9–10; 6:7,9; 11:19–20; 31:10–13; Ps. 78:5–8; 2 Chron. 17:7–9; Dan. 1:3–21; Matt. 6:25–30; 1 Cor. 12:28; Gal. 3:24–25; Eph. 4:11; 2 Tim. 1:11; 2:2.

Local State, and Federal Governments and Judicial System: Mayor, city council, police, firemen, welfare offices, foster care personnel, state and federal congressmen, governor, president, vice-president, cabinet, judges, federal judges, and state and federal supreme court justices.

Matt. 22:17–21; Luke 20:25; Rom. 13:1–7; Titus 3:1; 1 Pet. 2:13–17.

Medical Community: Doctors, nurses, ambulance personnel, hospital staff and administrators.

Jer. 8:22; 30:13; Luke 10:34; Rev. 22:2.

Business: Honesty, integrity, fair pricing, good employee relationships.

Lev. 25:43; Deut. 5:14; 24:14–15; Job 31:13–15; Prov. 22:16; 29:21; Jer. 22:13; Mal. 3:5; Matt. 10:10; 20:1–15; Luke 10:7; Rom. 4:4; Eph. 6:9; Col. 4:1; 1 Tim. 5:18; Philem. 15; Jas. 5:4–5.

Sports Figures: Be good role models.

Lev. 18:2–3; Deut. 18:9; 2 Chron. 30:7; Prov. 22:24; Isa. 8:11; Jer. 16:12; 17:1; Ezek. 20:18; Hos. 4:9, 15; Matt. 23:1–3; 1 Cor. 8:9–13; 10:6; Eph. 4:17; 3 John 11; Neh. 5:8–19; Ps. 101:2; 1 Thess. 1:6; 1 Tim. 4:12; Tit. 2:7–8; Heb. 13:7; 1 Pet. 1:13,17; 2:11–25; 3:5; 5:3.

Media: Radio, TV, newspaper, magazine, fairness (no bias), honesty, and accuracy in reporting.

Hab. 1:13; Prov. 27:20; Eccl. 1:8; 1 Thess. 5:4–6,21; 1 John 2:16.

Other Churches: Unity, purity in message, growth, financial blessing staying in the center of God's will, purity for all leadership and the congregation, evangelistic messages.

Ps. 133:1; Isa. 52:8; Matt. 23:8; Acts 4:32; Rom. 12:16; 14:19; 15:5; 1 Cor. 1:10; 2 Cor. 13:11; Eph. 4:3; Phil. 1:27; 2:2; 3:16; 1 Pet. 3:8; Heb. 3:13; 10:24; 1 John 1:3,7.

Criminal Element: Their salvation—through radio, TV, neighbor, or other person who will reach out and help these needy people to come to salvation and the lordship of Jesus; God to supply their needs so they will not desire to use negative means to accomplish their purposes; They will find no satisfaction in their way of life.

Ezek. 22:8–12; 27-30; Hos. 4:1–2; Matt. 15:19; Rom. 1:24, 29–32; 3:14–18; 1 Cor. 5:11; Gal. 5:19–21.

Occult: Those involved will see how dangerous it is and want to get out; they will come to salvation; God's protection of His children against those involved in the occult who might want to do them harm.

Lev. 19:26–28,31; 20:6; Deut. 18:9–14; Isa. 8:19; Mal. 3:5; Ezek. 12:23–24; 13:23; Micah 5:12; 3:7; Gal. 5:20; 1 Sam. 5:23; Ex. 22:18; Lev. 20:27.

Pornography: Movies, bookstores, lewd nightclubs, prostitution, deviant sexual lifestyles—salvation of those who own and participate in these things.

Ex. 20:17; Job 31:9–12; Ps. 81:12; Prov. 6:24–25; Matt. 5:28; Mark 4:19; John 8:44; 1 Cor. 9:27; 10:6–7; Eph. 4:22; 1 Tim. 6:9; 2 Tim. 2:22; 4:3; Titus 2:12; Jas. 1:14; 4:1–3; 1 Pet. 2:18; 3:3; 1 John 2:16–17; Jude 16,18.

Pastoral Prayer Team

Pastoral prayer teams are an important way to provide the pastor and his family with a prayer covering that can be used to launch all activities in their ministry. C. Peter Wagner writes:

> I am convinced that most church members have little or no appreciation of the cost of being a pastor. They know what their pastor looks like and sounds like on the outside, but they have little more idea of what is happening on the inside than they have about what is happening on the inside of their digital watch they look at many times a day. (*Prayer Shield*, 61)

The ideal organization of a pastoral prayer team would include the selection of thirty-one men who will commit long-term (at least one year) to a process of learning and growing in the area of prayer. After a period of orientation and learning, each would be assigned a specific day of each month to pray. Obviously, if there are fewer men, those involved may have to double up. But, nonetheless, you begin with whatever amount of prayer warriors the Lord has directed to you.

For instance, if the Lord directs seven men to the pastor, each man would be involved one day each week for each month. On every Sunday morning, the seven men who have been praying for the pastor throughout the week would meet with him before the worship service(s) to pray for him. They may also choose to pray during the service for their week of commitment. Several things can take place in this weekly exchange:

- Exchange prayer requests and answers to prayer.

- Prayer for specific areas of concern in the pastor's ministry or family.
- Have the pastor kneel and pray God's blessing upon him while laying hands upon him.
- Pray for power and protection for the upcoming service(s).
- Pray for open hearts, for the people to be receptive to what God has placed upon the pastor's heart to share.
- Pray for wisdom and the mind of Christ for the pastor as he faces the new week of ministry and the encouragement he needs when facing difficult decisions.
- Ask for energy and stamina to be able to accomplish all he has to do in the coming week and the ability to priortize his schedule.
- Ask the Lord to give him wise counsel and friendships.
- Pray that he will look only to God for approval and not to man.

For an entire year, this format will provide constant prayer support for the pastor providing the foundational power for his personal and corporate ministry.

A variety of variations may appear more appropriate to your situation, but the incorporation of the following key ingredients will bring greater effectiveness and unity in this ministry.

- Share a picture of the person and his family to focus the prayer time.
- Meet once a year at a prayer retreat to refresh and learn more about individual and corporate prayer.
- Ask God to give the team a close relationship, a bonding in Christian unity and concern.
- Send notes of encouragement. Become a Barnabas.
- Have the prayer team individuals include their own families in the praying events.
- Commit to reading one book on prayer each year as a team.

Remember, "the effective prayer of a righteous man can accomplish much" (Jas. 5:16, NASB).

How to Solve Prayer Problems

Prayer problems fall into two major categories: things that are wrong in your attitudes, and actions or things that can interfere with your concentration and hinder the effectiveness of your times with the Lord.

Attitudes and Actions Which Hinder Prayer

- Wanting your own will, not God's.
- Selfishness and wrong motives (Jas. 4:2–3).
- Unforgiving spirit (Matt. 5:23–24).
- Lack of compassion (Prov. 21:13).
- Lack of domestic harmony or peace with mate, children, relatives (1 Pet. 3:7).
- Pride (Job 35:12–13).
- Disobedience (1 John 3:22).
- Lack of faith (Jas. 5:15).
- Failure to ask according to God's will (1 John 5:14).
- Failure to know God's Word and abide in Christ (John 15:7).
- Hypocrisy (Matt. 6:5).
- Wrong attitudes; e.g., impure thoughts, jealousy, guilt, worry, discouragement, critical spirit, frustration, or aimlessness.
- Loss of first love (Rev. 2:4).
- Lukewarmness (Rev. 3:16).
- Critical attitude (Matt. 7:1–5).

Following are several suggested sample prayers that address personal shortcomings. Modify them to suit your needs.

A prayer for dealing with self-doubt:

> Father, You know my heart. I sometimes fail to recognize the enemy's voice and think it is my own thoughts that are accusing me of these things. Please help me to remember that it is Satan who is the accuser of the brethren, that he wants me to doubt You and to doubt myself, that it is he who brings up my past, my failures and shortcomings to me. Help me not to listen to him anymore. Holy Spirit, remind me when a thought comes that is not from You. Show me how to resist it.

A prayer for dealing with the sin you cannot overcome:

> Father, I know _____is a sin and grieves Your heart, yet I have tried to stop so many times and failed. I know it does not honor You to continue and that You want me to stop. So if I'm ever going to stop _____, You are going to have to give me the ability and willpower. So I'm asking that the next time I am tempted to _____, that You, Holy Spirit, will remind me that this is a sin and then give me the courage and power to resist the temptation to _____.

A prayer to let go of past pain:

> Father, It is sometimes so difficult to know how to handle_____. Show me how to think about it. What scriptural principle(s) should I be applying? You know how hurt I get in such situations. You know how difficult it is for me to stop thinking about what has happened. Help! I need Your control, Your perspective.

Overcoming Hindrances to Prayer

If Prayer Seems Boring...

• Ask God to:
—show you how to have variety and help you to enjoy it.
—show you anything you may be doing that is wrong and any unconfessed sin that is interfering.
—restore your first love. Ask Him to make your heart long after Him like David's heart.
—help you draw near to Him. The closer you are to Him, the more meaningful your times will be with Him. (See Jas. 4:8.)
—minister to you each time you read the Word. Look for at least one fresh truth, insight, or application to your life.

• Go to your time with God *expecting* to enjoy it.

• Read books on prayer to learn different elements to include. See resource 4.

- Look at resource 2 for ideas.

- Ask others what they are doing that is helpful.

- Get at least one other person—spouse, friend, prayer partner—to pray about it.

- Recognize that the enemy is going to do everything he can to get you to stop. Telling you it is boring is one of his tricks. Review the materials on page 10.

- Make this your *highest priority*. Determine that this is the most important thing of the day, more important than sleep, than eating, than entertainment (like TV or games) or even an individual.

If Time Is Hard To Find...

- Claim the promise that if you seek God and His kingdom first, He will give to you the things you need (Matt. 6:33).

- Ask God to show you how and when to have your time together. Realize He wants this even more than you do.

- Realize also that Satan does not want you to have any time with God. He will whisper to you whatever excuse he can get you to accept as valid.

- If possible, go to bed earlier so you can get up earlier. The undisturbed quiet hours of the morning, before you face your day, are your "prime time" prayer hours.

- Less desirable but necessary for busy people is to split your time into two or three parts. This limits the time to flow into a more intimate relationship, but it does provide time with the Lord and He will bless your effort and the desire of your heart. Many mothers find that after a while the Lord helps them focus more quickly and the time is even more rewarding. For a busy mother, the best times might be before the children get up, during their naps, while they are watching cartoons, or after they go to bed.

- Ask God to show you how. Commit to having a significant daily time with the Lord. Read Psalm 42 and 119.

How to Make It Meaningful...

- Do the Two-week Enrichment, resource 2.

- Continue having a regular quiet time upon completion of the above solution. During this time, read one or more of the books in resource 4 under the heading "Quiet Time Helps."

- Ask others what they do that works.

- Try the format in Dick Eastman's book, *The Hour that Changes the World*, or that of Larry Lea's *Could You Not Tarry One Hour?*

- Ask the Lord to show you how to avoid distractions.

Distractions...

- Pray each time before you start that the Lord will keep away any distractions and help you to concentrate on Him.

- Is there a better time or place to have it? Consider early morning before family is up or phones are ringing. This may mean going to bed earlier. If you are not a morning person, ask the Lord to change you if He wants you to have your time with Him in the early morning.

- The clock can sometimes prove a distraction if you must hurry your time with the Lord before going somewhere. People who can fall asleep easily could rise very early—5 A.M.—even 4 A.M.—have their time with the Lord for as long as they wish (the clock usually is not a factor), and then go back to bed until time to get up.

- Have a paper and pen so you can jot down anything you need to do. Once on paper, those thoughts should no longer interrupt you and you will remember them too.

- If children interrupt, try to have your quiet time during their nap or tell them that when you are in your quiet time place with your Bible, they are to leave you alone. Have something self-entertaining for them to do at that time. If you are fortunate enough to have a Christian neighbor with kids, you might consider watching each other's children during quiet times.

- Telephone interruptions can be handled by answering machine or by letting people know that each day you will be unavailable to answer the telephone, even if you are home, during the specified time You could take the phone off the hook, but be certain to put it back. This may mean a reminder card you keep with your Bible.

If It Is Hard to Concentrate...

- Pray before starting, asking the Lord to help you concentrate, to touch your heart and make it so interesting you will stay focused.

- Try journaling. (See resources 2 and 19, sample #3.) Many believers find writing out at least their praise, worship, confession, and dedication of themselves makes it is easier to stay focused. Requests don't seem that difficult to remember or do.

- Have some organization to your quiet time so you know what you will be doing next.

Survey of
Individual Prayer Skills

Note: The following is only a sample. This will need to be adapted to your specific church prayer opportunities.

	Yes	No	I wish this were true
Willing			
1. I regularly attend week-night prayer meetings.	☐	☐	☐
2. I regularly attend the Men's/Women's Prayer Break fast.	☐	☐	☐
3. I enjoy praying out loud with other people.	☐	☐	☐
4. I have put into practice some of the things I am learning about prayer.	☐	☐	☐
5. I wish I could spend more time in prayer.	☐	☐	☐
Intercessor			
6. I pray by myself for one or more hours each day.	☐	☐	☐
7. I have read one or more books on prayer in the last year.	☐	☐	☐
8. I enjoy the challenge of praying for others.	☐	☐	☐
9. I regularly see answers to prayer.	☐	☐	☐
10. I have a specific time set aside for prayer each day and am consistent in using that time for prayer.	☐	☐	☐
11. To the best of my ability, I let nothing interfere in my prayer time.	☐	☐	☐
Burdened			
12. I often find I have a deep burden to pray for things I hear from others and from church.	☐	☐	☐

13. I am involved in a small group and participate in the prayer times. . . . . □   □   □

14. I have attended one or more prayer conferences in the last three years. (Write down names of conferences.). . . . . . . □   □   □

15. At times tears may come to my eyes or I may get upset with things I hear about on the news. These cause me to ask the Lord to intervene and change things.. . . . . □   □   □

16. I regularly pray for our missionaries. . . . . □   □   □

Prayer Warrior/Spiritual Warrior

17. Prayer is a difficult and boring thing, but I do it because I know I should and feel a strong burden to do so. . . . . □   □   □

18. I often seem to know what Satan is trying to do in a given situation and take that insight to prayer. . . . . □   □   □

19. When I am praying, I often lose track of time . . . . □   □   □

20. When I am praying it sometimes is as though the Lord shows me exactly what to say about the topic. . . . . □   □   □

21. At times I get so angry or concerned at what Satan is trying to do to stop God's work or hurt people, that I either address him directly and demand in the name of Jesus that he stop his activity or I ask the Lord to do so. . . . . □   □   □

22. It is not unusual for me to wake up in the middle of the night with a burden to pray for a specific person. . . . . . . □   □   □

Now that you have completed this survey, please answer the following questions:

- Do you feel satisfied with your prayer skills as they are?
- Would you like to learn more about prayer so you could in the future be able to respond in the affirmative to more of these questions?
- Is there anything you would like to tell us about your feelings toward prayer or how God is moving in your heart at this time concerning prayer?

Evaluating Pray-ers

By looking at each person's completed survey (resource 14) and the explanations below, you should be able to determine a person's desire to pray, as well as praying skills. You can then use this information to utilize the person more fully in your prayer needs. At the same time you can encourage the individual to grow more in the areas of will and skill. If you find it unclear, then talk further with the individual to clarify which category comes closest to describing him or her.

W—*Willing* to pray for church needs but not overly so; open to training in prayer.

I—*Intercessor* has a higher level of commitment to prayer than the willing person but does not have a compelling burden. He may be young in his intercessory skills or simply has not gone beyond a certain level of prayer commitment. He believes in prayer and has seen God use him through prayer but is not yet absorbed by it.

B—*Burdened* to pray for church needs; often frustrated at lack of time to pray or at lack of prayer in others.

PW—*Prayer warrior* knows and uses the principles of spiritual warfare but does not spend regularly large quantities of time in prayer. However, his personal prayer life will be strong and consistent.

SW—*Spiritual warrior* spends at least one to two hours a day in prayer. It may not all be for the church. Has consistent prayer life and spends much of his time in intercession and spiritual warfare praying both offensively and defensively against the enemy's attacks. This person is usually very sensitive to God's leading and will.

How to Pray for Your Pastor and His Family*

You should have the following general attitude in praying for your pastor, and all your Christian leaders for that matter.

Therefore encourage one another, and build up one another, just as you also are doing. But we request of you brethren, that you appreciate those who diligently labor among you, and have charge over you in the Lord and give you instruction, and that you esteem them very highly in love because of their work. Live in peace with one another (1 Thess. 5:11–13).**

I thank my God in all remembrance of you, always offering prayer with joy in my every prayer for you all, in view of your participation in the gospel (Phil. 1:3–5).

Pray the following Scriptures for Your pastor by putting his name (or his family's name) into the verses where appropriate and making the verse a specific request.

Relationship with God

Pray that he will…

- *Be a man after God's own heart.*

    A man after My heart, who will do all My will (Acts 13:22).

    As the deer pants for the water brooks, So my soul pants for Thee, O God (Ps. 42:1).

- *Be a man of the Word.*

    O how I love Thy law! It is my meditation all the day (Ps. 119:97).

*Resources 16 A–K, and M were developed by Prayerworks, a division of Campus Crusade for Christ.
**Scriptures in Resources 16A and B are from the *New American Standard Bible.*

Let the word of Christ richly dwell within you, with all wisdom, teaching and admonishing one another with psalms and hymns and spiritual songs, singing with thankfulness in your hearts to God (Col. 3:16).

Thy word I have treasured in my heart, that I may not sin against Thee (Ps. 119:11).

- *Allow God to direct his every step.*

The steps of a man are established by the Lord (Ps. 37:23).

- *Have a growing, deepening relationship with God in prayer.*

Delight yourself in the Lord; and He will give you the desires of your hearts (Ps. 37:4).

O God, Thou art my God; I shall seek Thee earnestly; my soul thirsts for Thee, my flesh yearns for Thee, in a dry and weary land where there is no water...My soul clings to Thee; Thy right hand upholds me (Ps. 63:1, 8).

- *Be a spirit-filled man of faith and love.*

For this reason, I bow my knees before the Father . . . that He would grant you . . . to be strengthened with power through His Spirit in the inner man; so that Christ may dwell in your hearts through faith; and that you, being rooted and grounded in love, may be able to comprehend . . . and to know the love of Christ which surpasses knowledge, that you may be filled up to all the fullness of God (Eph. 3:14–19).

- *Have good health, strength, and endurance.*

Family Relationships

Pray that...

- *Family members are loving, unselfish, respectful, and understanding.*

Husbands, love your wives, just as Christ also loved the church and gave Himself up for her (Eph. 5:25).

You husbands likewise, live with your wives in an understanding way (1 Pet. 3:7).

Nevertheless let each individual among you also love his own wife even as himself; and let the wife see to it that she respect her husband (Eph. 5:33).

Children obey your parents in the Lord. Honor your father and mother (Eph. 6:1–2).

Fathers, do not provoke your children to anger; but bring them up in the discipline and instruction of the Lord (Eph. 6:4).

- *The family is a source of joy and blessing to one another.*

The father of the righteous will greatly rejoice, and he who begets a wise son will be glad in him (Prov. 23:24).

A woman who fears the Lord, she shall be praised. Her children rise up and bless her; her husband also, and he praises her (Prov. 31:30 28).

A righteous man who walks in his integrity—How blessed are his sons after him (Prov. 20:7).

- *They will have God's constant protection and peace.*

Ministry

Pray that he will. . .

- *Be devoted to prayer and the Word.*

But we will devote ourselves to prayer, and to the ministry of the word (Acts 6:4).

- *Intercede for and instruct his congregation.* Pray that he will know the hearts of his people and their needs and be able to pray for them and minister to them accordingly.

Moreover, as for me, far be it from me that I should sin against the Lord by ceasing to pray for you; but I will instruct you in the good and right way (1 Sam. 12:23).

For God . . . is my witness as to how unceasingly I make mention of you always in my prayers (Rom. 1:9–10)

- *Have a fruitful ministry.*

You did not choose Me, but I chose you and appointed you, that you should go and bear fruit, and that your fruit should remain, that whatever you ask of the Father in My name, He may give to you (John 15:16).

And we proclaim Him, admonishing every man and teaching every man with all wisdom, that we may present every man complete in Christ (Col. 1:28).

Pray that...
—He will be able to handle with grace and patience, the many responsibilities he has.

—He will be sensitive to the leading of the Lord both as he prepares and as he speaks, resulting in the Holy Spirit speaking to us through the message.

—He will have a strong, close, harmonious working relationship with those in leadership.

—The Lord will give him insights into the solution for problems.

—He will know how to counsel those who come to him for advice and help.

- *Equip the saints for service and discipleship.*

  And He gave some as...pastors and teachers, for the equipping of the saints for the work of service to the building up of the body of Christ (Eph. 4:11–12).

  And the things which you have heard from me in the presence of many witnesses, these entrust to faithful men, who will be able to teach others also (2 Tim. 2:2).

- *Be protected from the evil one.*

  Finally, brethren, pray for us that the word of the Lord may spread rapidly and be glorified . . . that we may be delivered from perverse and evil men; for not all have faith. But the Lord is faithful, and He will strengthen and protect you from the evil one (2 Thess. 3:1–3).

Relationship with Church

Pray that...

- *The congregation will pray regularly for him and his family.*
- *The congregation will respect and guard as much as possible his time with his family, especially in the early mornings, evenings, and weekends.*
- *The congregation will not impose standards on his children they do not expect from other children.*

How to Pray
For a Worship Service

But an hour is coming, and now is, when the true worshipers shall worship the Father in spirit and truth; for such people the Father seeks to be His worshipers (John 4:23).

The following are prayer topics that will strengthen your worship service. Pray that:

- The worship time will be glorifying to God.
- Our hearts will be prepared to hear from God so that He can speak to each person present through the music and message.
- The pastor will be sensitive to the leading of the Lord both as he prepares and as he speaks, resulting in the Holy Spirit speaking to us through the message.
- People will be faithful to apply to their lives what God shows them during the service.
- People will come to the Lord both for salvation and renewal.
- The musicians will each be in good voice and show forth the joy of the Lord.
- God will give wisdom and guidance for those choosing the music, that each song will deepen our worship experience and prepare us for the message.
- All equipment will work perfectly.
- All who attend will feel the love of God in our people and sense a spirit of peace and unity and that they are an important part of our church.

- Visitors will feel welcomed, be ministered to, and will desire to become part of our church family.

O come, let us sing for joy to the Lord; let us shout joyfully to the rock of our salvation. let us come before His presence with thanksgiving; let us shout joyfully to Him with psalms. For the Lord is a great God, and a great King above all gods . . . Come let us worship and bow down; let us kneel before the Lord our Maker. For He is our God, and we are the people of His pasture, and the sheep of His hand (Ps. 95:1–3, 6–7).

How to Intercede for Your Church Finances

God's Viewpoint on Giving and Your Finances

Note: The prayers in this resource are given as samples of what would be appropriate to pray for under each principle. They are offered as a tool. You may want either to pray them as they are, making them your own because you are in agreement, or else pray the concepts in your own words.

Scriptural Principle #1

Give to God not only because He deserves it for all He has done for you, but because it is His command. When you do, then He promises He will meet all your needs and will pour out His blessings on your lives.

Render therefore unto Caesar the things which are Caesar's; and unto God the things that are God's (Matt. 22:21, KJV).

Will a man rob God? Yet you rob me. But you ask, How do we rob you? In tithes and offerings. You are under a curse . . . because you are robbing me. Bring the whole tithe into the storehouse, that there may be food in my house. Test me in this, says the Lord Almighty, and see if I will not throw open the floodgates of heaven and pour out so much blessing that you will not have room enough for it (Mal. 3:8–10).

God will meet all your needs according to his glorious riches in Christ Jesus (Phil. 4:19).

- Ask the Lord to give each member the courage to do just what He has said: to test Him through giving at least a tithe (10 percent) of his gross income to the Lord, even though it may seem impossible.

- In turn, thank the Lord that He will honor His promise in His Word to pour out a blessing on the individual.

Pray that each person's motives for giving to the Lord will be pure and not just to receive a blessing.

- Ask that as God pours out His blessings, whether material or spiritual, the person receiving them will recognize that they are from God and are given because of his obedience in giving.

- Request that tithing and giving will become a way of life with each individual so that there can never be any opportunity for the enemy successfully to tempt you not to give on any occasion because of circumstances.

Scriptural Principle #2

Giving should come from a cheerful, generous, appreciative heart in love with God.

Whoever sows sparingly will also reap sparingly, and whoever sows generously will also reap generously. Each man should give what he has decided in his heart to give, not reluctantly or under compulsion, for God loves a cheerful giver. And God is able to make all grace abound to you, so that in all things at all times, having all that you need, you will abound in every good work (2 Cor. 9:6–8).

Pray that your church family members will be so in love with the Lord, so wanting to please Him, that they will see giving to Him through the church as a privilege and joy, and that they will give "generously." Ask the Lord to help them see this as a privilege and not something done only out of obligation.

Scriptural Principle #3

Your tithe should be the first thing you pay.

Honor the Lord with your wealth, with the first fruits of all your crops; then your barns will be filled to overflowing and your vats will brim over with new wine (Prov. 3:9).

Upon the first day of the week, let every one of you lay by him in store, as God has prospered him (1 Cor. 16:2).

Lord, help me to give You my tithe from my paycheck as soon I get it rather than paying all my bills and giving to You if there is any left over. Help each one of us in the church to do this so as to be obedient and pleasing to You. Help us to trust You to meet all our needs when we do this, even though we do not know from where the money will come to do so. Remind us how faithful You are to Your Word and promises. Enable us also to be able to give You gifts over and above our tithes with thankful, rejoicing hearts, so that the enemy will not be able to make us feel like we are "sacrificing" in order to give to You.

Scriptural Principle #4

God evaluates your giving based on your heart and ability to give, not on the amount given.

The widow's small coins in Mark 12:42 are seen by Jesus as being more important than the many that the rich give which cost them little. So *nothing is too small.*

For I testify that they gave as much as they were able, and even beyond their ability (2 Cor. 8:3).

Pray that you will see all tithes and gifts to the Lord as important and never let the enemy trick you out of a blessing by telling you what you have is too little to count or that you simply cannot afford to give your tithe. Ask the Lord to remind you of Jesus' teaching on this when such a temptation comes to you. Pray that you will give generously.

Scriptural Principle #5

Money can be used either for good or for evil.

For the love of money is a root of all kinds of evil. Some people, eager for money, have wandered from the faith and pierced themselves with many griefs. Command those who are rich in this present world not to be arrogant nor to put their hope in wealth, which is so uncertain, but to put their hope in God, who richly provides us with everything for our enjoyment. Command them to do good, to be rich in good deeds, and to be generous and willing to share. In this way they will lay up treasure for themselves as a firm foundation for the coming age, so that they may take hold of the life that is truly life (1 Tim. 6:6; 10;17–19).

Lord, help us hold money lightly and not let it own us. Let You be our only God, not love for money or what it can buy. Let us be as generous with our money as You are with us. Help us invest in what counts for eternity. Give us wisdom in how we spend our monies. Help us be content with what we have and not be looking for what we can buy, or how to "keep up with the Joneses."

A Sample Closing Prayer

Lord, help us to be good examples to all around us of how we manage our monies, both as individuals within the church, and as a church. Let the offerings always be sufficient to cover all needs. Give wisdom to those making our budgets to know how much should be asked for during the year. Help us to spend it wisely. Show us how to take advantage of any bargains or discounts that may be available to us, both as a church and for our own families.

Help our children to catch a vision for not being too impressed with money or with things; let them see the importance through our example of giving to You what You deserve and desire. Help all of us to realize that You do not need our money, but rather are giving us the privilege of giving You another opportunity to pour out blessings on us in response to our obedience. May we never take Your resultant blessings for granted. Help our giving always to be cheerful and from a heart of love for You.

How to Pray For Missions

Note: The following is presented in an extended version to fit most mission situations. Choose only those points which apply to the particular situation for which you are praying. Often background information is included for a better picture of the situation.

The Mission Field

Local/National Governments

- Pray that they will not be resistant to Christianity, and will allow evangelizing and conversions.

- Ask God to keep the doors open so missionaries can continue to come in and that new doors will be opened to allow more opportunities to share. (For example, if the only access to the country is through tent making, then ask the Lord to change the laws and, until that time, allow the missionaries to stay in a suitable job.)

  Pray for us, too, that God may open a door for our message, so that we may proclaim the mystery of Christ (Col. 4:3).

- Pray that high level officials will come to the Lord and be willing to help make any necessary changes.

- Ask the Lord to give believing officials wisdom to know with whom to share their faith.

Unsaved Nationals

- Pray that they will become dissatisfied with their present form of worship.

- Pray that many questions will disturb them that could eventually lead them to salvation.

- Pray that God will prepare the "soil" of their heart.

- Pray that God will keep Satan from blinding them to the truth. (See Matt. 13:19; 2 Cor. 4:4.)

Saved Nationals Pray that:

- They will be willing to openly profess their faith in Christ and to face whatever opposition may come.
- There will be a good working relationship with the missionaries.
- God will raise up godly men to provide strong leadership for the Christian community, especially for church men of the Word and willing to make whatever sacrifices are necessary to lead the people.
- God will supply all of their financial and spiritual needs.
- God will give them a hunger and thirst for His Word.
- They will understand the difference between their old religion and the God of the Bible, as well as any other misconceptions. (Usually their own gods are not loving, kind or merciful, so even though they embrace Jehovah God, they may tend to transfer to Him the characteristics of previous gods. They may also see Him as being limited in power and not present everywhere. Salvation may also be seen as a "work," even though they are taught otherwise. God's ability to work all things for good or to keep them safe may be a hard concept for them to accept.)

Missionaries

Asking God to fill you with the knowledge of his will through all spiritual wisdom and understanding . . . that you may live a life worthy of the Lord and may please him in every way: bearing fruit in every good work, growing in the knowledge of God, being strengthened with all power according to his glorious might so that you may have great endurance and patience, and joyfully giving thanks to the Father (Col. 1:9–14).

Prayer Covering at Home Pray that God will raise up members of your congregation to form a strong prayer covering for the missionary. Also ask God to help the people on the prayer team be faithful in praying consistently and specifically. Ask the Lord to help the team leader keep his pray-ers well informed of both prayer requests and praises.

For those working in sensitive areas, pray for wisdom for them to be able to know how to communicate prayer requests and that God will keep such communications out of the hands of those who might want to stop their ministry.

Pray the missionaries will adjust to the culture, language, and the people and not become critical or feel superior.

Adjustments and Attitudes

- There probably are differing standards of cleanliness, of time usage, medical practices, moral and value systems, and availability of necessities.

- Ask God to give them great patience in all circumstances.

- Ask God to help them function with government agencies without violating their Christian ethical standards and without becoming critical of those who do compromise. (Bribing is often a way of life.)

- They will have favor with the nationals. There will be good two-way communication between nationals and missionaries with no misunderstandings coming from language or cultural differences. (Too often the Westerner is seen as trying to impose his values and methods on the nationals, and sometimes this is true. The missionary needs a sensitivity to the Lord to know what values he holds that should be transferred [such as no longer allowing polygamous marriages to occur, but not breaking up ones already established before salvation] and which ones are non-essentials [such as the style of worship].)

- Pray the Lord will give them grace and a sweet spirit to eat whatever is offered to them, will keep them healthy even when the food is not clean, and that they will not do anything to offend culturally.

- Ask the Lord to build a strong bond between the missionaries and the people they are serving, and that they will have a good insight into people.

A Deep, Unconditional Love

- Intercede that the missionary will be humble and will think of the nationals as "better than themselves" and that they will have a true servant's heart.

I make myself a slave to everyone to win as many as possible (1 Cor. 9:19).

Do nothing out of selfish ambition or vain conceit, but in humility consider others better than yourselves. Each of you should look not only to your own interests, but also to the interests of others (Phil. 2:3–4).

- Pray that the missionaries would be persons after God's own heart and that their relationship with God will remain strong and always growing.

Their Relationship with God

A man after My heart, who will do all My will (Acts 13:22, NASB).

As the deer pants for the water brooks, so my soul pants for Thee, O God (Ps. 42:1).

• The missionaries will be students of the Word.

O how I love Thy law! It is my meditation all the day (Ps. 119:97, NASB).

Let the word of Christ richly dwell within you, with all wisdom, teaching and admonishing one another with psalms and hymns and spiritual songs, singing with thankfulness in your hearts to God (Col. 3:16).

Your word have I treasured in my heart, that I may not sin against you (Ps. 119:11, NASB).

• The missionaries will seek the Lord's guidance for every detail of their life and will allow God to direct their every step.

The steps of a man are established by the Lord (Ps. 37:23, NASB).

• Their prayer life will grow and deepen.

Delight yourself in the Lord; and He will give you the desires of your hearts (Ps 37:4, NASB).

O God, Thou art my God; I shall seek Thee earnestly; my soul thirst for Thee, my flesh yearns for Thee, in a dry and weary land where there is no water. My soul clings to Thee; Thy right hand upholds me (Ps. 63:1,8, NASB).

• They will walk in strong faith and love.

For this reason, I bow my knees before the Father . . . that He would grant you . . . to be strengthened with power through His Spirit in the inner man; so that Christ may dwell in your hearts through faith; and that you, being rooted and grounded in love, may be able to comprehend . . . and to know the love of Christ which surpass knowledge, that you may be filled to all the fullness of God (Eph. 3:14, 16–19, NASB).

• That the missionaries will keep their eyes on the Lord and not their circumstances.

God's Will and Perspective

• Pray for them to know God's will and to be sensitive to Him as He shows them His strategy for their ministry and in reaching the people.

• Ask the Lord to give them courage to do all that He shows them and not be intimidated by anyone or anything.

- Pray that the missionaries have the anointing of the Lord on their ministry, with His words being spoken through them to all with whom they talk.

- Pray that they will disciple consistently.

- Ask that they recognize that as long as they are ministering in God's will, they are successful and should rejoice, and that someday there will be a harvest for Him.

- Pray they will share their faith obediently as the Lord leads.

The man who plants and the man who waters have one purpose, and each will be rewarded according to his own labor. For we are God's fellow workers (1 Cor. 3:8–9).

For we walk by faith, not by sight (2 Cor. 5:7, NASB).

Good Health

- Ask God to give the missionaries strength and the ability to withstand the pressures of living on the front lines of the "battle," as well as a healthy emotional outlook.

Endure hardship with us like a good soldier of Christ Jesus ...Therefore I endure everything for the sake of the elect, that they too may obtain the salvation that is in Christ Jesus (2 Tim. 2:3, 10).

- Pray that they will keep a positive attitude toward all situations and circumstances and will resist all doubt, fear, and discouragement or any other temptations.

- Ask God to keep all medical treatment accurate and safe. (Sterilization of equipment is not always sufficient.)

Unity with Other Missionaries

(This is often a problem on the mission field. The enemy can bring problems among the staff and between the nationals and missionaries.)

Pray that there will be a oneness of mind among the missionaries; that they will each be willing to accept the imperfections in each other as well as in the nation; that they will not set their standards so high that they become critical.

I urge you to live a life worthy of the calling you have received. Be completely humble and gentle; be patient, bearing with one another in love. Make every effort to keep the unity of the Spirit through the bond of peace (Eph. 4:1–3).

Contentment

Ask God to give missionaries contentment in their circumstances—housing, food, transportation, weather, and medical facilities.

I have learned to be content whatever the circumstances (Phil. 4:11).

| God's Supernatural Protection | Ask that God's protection of the believers be very evident to all. (Often times there are natural disasters—floods, hurricanes, volcanic action, earthquakes, famines, wars, etc.) |

Holidays or Special Occasions

Pray that special days will not be a low time for them as they are away from their loved ones and homeland. Pray for local celebrations among other expatriates to be satisfying.

(Ask the Lord to help them see this as a positive sacrifice they are making for Him. Pray that they will rejoice that they can make such a sacrifice.)

Sufficient Finances

My God shall supply all your needs according to His riches in Christ Jesus (Phil. 4:19, KJV).

Spending Money

Pray that they will spend their money wisely, especially in front of nationals. Westerners always have more money than nationals, so it can be a stumbling block to the national if he perceives the westerner is rich while he is poor.

Peace About Home Concerns

Ask God to help the missionaries leave any concerns such as aging parents or illnesses that occur while they are on the field, in the hands of the Lord.

Leave all your worries with Him because He cares for you (1 Pet. 5:7, TEV).

Patience, Understanding, and Forgiveness

• Ask God to give them a right understanding about differences in culture and people, and help them avoid misunderstandings.

• Be able to accept weaknesses in people and love them anyway.

• Cope with frustrating occurrences and shortages of supplies.

• Accept, without complaining, delays in government as well as ministry transactions.

Miscellaneous Requests

Pray that all equipment, including automobiles and appliances, will run well and not break down. If repair parts ever are needed, pray that they will be able to get them. Ask the Lord to supply all necessities and keep them available (for example, telephones, electricity and water).

Pray that packages sent to missionaries will get through without stealing, breakage, or undue customs charges.

The Husband and Wife Team

Strong Relationships

• Pray that each member will be loving, unselfish, respectful, understanding, honoring, and cooperative.

Husbands, love your wives, just as Christ loved the church and gave himself up for her (Eph. 5:25).

You husbands likewise, live with your wives in an understanding way (1 Pet. 3:7, NASB)

Nevertheless let each individual among you also love his own wife even as himself; and let the wife see to it that she respect her husband (Eph. 5:33, NASB)

Children, obey your parents in the Lord...honor your father and mother (Eph. 6:1,2, NASB)

Fathers, do not provoke your children to anger, but bring them up in the discipline and instruction of the Lord (Eph. 6:4, NASB).

- Family members will be a source of joy to one another.

The father of the righteous will greatly rejoice, and he who begets a wise son will be glad in him (Prov. 23:24, NASB).

A woman who fears the Lord, she shall be praised. Her children rise up and bless her; her husband also, and he praises her (Prov. 31:30, 28, NASB).

A righteous man who walks in his integrity—How blessed are his sons after him (Prov. 20: 7, NASB).

- God will protect the family and give them good health, His joy, and peace in all circumstances.

I will say of the Lord, "He is my refuge and my fortress, my God, in whom I trust." Surely he will save you from the fowler's snare and from the deadly pestilence . . . You will not fear the terror of night, nor the arrow that flies by day, nor the pestilence that stalks in the darkness, nor the plague that destroys at midday. A thousand may fall at your side, ten thousand at your right hand, but it will not come near you (Ps. 91:2–3, 5–7).

I am the Lord that healeth thee (Ex. 15:26, KJV).

I pray that you may enjoy good health and that all may go well with you, even as your soul is getting along well (3 John 2).

- God will provide a good education for the children and give wisdom to know when and where they need to go away for further schooling.

The Single Person

Pray that the single missionaries will adjust to the culture and not be hampered by needs that cannot be met. (Sexual

Culture Adjustment

adjustment is often hard on some fields when one is there "for life" and there are no suitable prospects for marriage. (See Phil. 4:11.)

- Pray they will be content and will have no unfulfilled needs.
- Pray that God will help them see themselves as complete in Christ.

Future Spouse   Ask the Lord to prepare those who will eventually marry. Pray for patience and peace of mind, allowing God to show His choice of mate for them at the right time.

How to Pray
For an Unsaved Person

- Claim God's promise in 2 Peter 3:9 that He is not willing that any should perish but that all should come to repentance. Believe that because He is laying this person's salvation on your heart, that He is wanting him to be saved. Satan does not want you to pray for the person's salvation; only God would give you such a burden.

- Ask the Lord to do whatever is necessary to prepare the person's heart to hear, understand and accept the gospel when it is presented. (See Matt. 13:3–8. Ask God to till the soil of his heart's soil and fertilize it with His Word so he will become good soil.)

- Pray that the person will find no satisfaction in anything apart from God. (See Eccl. 1:2; 2:17.)

- Ask the Holy Spirit to draw the person to the Lord. (See John 6:44.)

- Ask God to bring a conviction of sin on the person. (See John 16:8.)

- Pray that the person will have a desire to change and live a holy life. (See Jas. 4:8, Heb. 10:22.)

If you know the person is living a self-righteous life, pray that the Holy Spirit will show him how he looks to God; i.e., his sinfulness and that good works cannot get them to heaven. (See Eph. 2:8,9; Isa. 64:6.)

- Request that the Lord answer any genuine questions or hang ups the person may have and that the person will accept the answer.

- Ask God to send someone or something to clearly communicate to the person Christ's claims; for example,

Christian radio or television, literature, someone at work, a relative, or yourself.

- Pray that the person will understand clearly who Jesus is and recognize his need for Christ as his Savior. (See Acts 4:12.)

- Ask God to let your life be a good testimony in front of the person. (See Matt. 5:16; 1 Cor. 11:1.)

- Pray that He will show you what you should say and when to say it, as well as when to be quiet. (See Isa. 30:21.)

- If the person has been very resistant to the gospel, ask the Lord to keep the enemy from interfering in his hearing and comprehending the gospel truths. In this way the next time the gospel is presented to him, he will have an opportunity to really understand and make an unhindered decision for or against Jesus, based on a true understanding of what is said. (See Isa. 35:5 ; 43:6–8.)

Remember: God says in James 5:16 that "the prayer of a righteous man is powerful and effective."

How to Intercede

Jesus Christ gave Himself on the cross as Intercessor for all men. Intercession is still His unceasing service and ministry to those who draw near to God through Him (Heb. 7:25).

Next to worship, intercession is the highest form of service you can perform. "The greatest thing anyone can do for God and man is to pray. It is not the only thing, but it is the chief thing" (S. D. Gordon, *Quiet Talks on Prayer*).

"Intercession is the link between man's impotence and God's omnipotence" (Andrew Murray).

An intercessor is one with genuine concern for others, who stands in the gap between man and God making requests before God or resisting the devil on man's behalf (See Ex. 32:9–14; Ps. 106:23; Ezek. 22:30–31; Jas. 4:7,8.)

As you come to God, you are requesting His hand to be moved on behalf of the person, nation, circumstance, and subject of your prayers. The enemy of men's souls is power-less against intercessory prayer.

You are directed by God's Word to intercede for others:

First of all, then, I urge that entreaties and prayers, petitions and thanksgivings, be made on behalf of all men, for kings and all who are in authority, in order that we may lead a tranquil and quiet life in all godliness and dignity. This is good and acceptable in the sight of God our Savior, who desires all men to be saved and to come to the knowledge of the truth (1 Tim. 2:1–4, NASB).

• Recognize that you are going into spiritual battle. It is essential, therefore, that you make certain there is nothing between you and God—no unconfessed sin, nothing you are holding back from His control. (See Isa. 59:2; 1 John 1:9.)

- Agree with Him that you are totally dependent upon the Holy Spirit to direct and energize your prayers. You need Him to guide you in how to pray for this person/situation. (See Rom 8:26.)

- God is concerned about everything. Pray believing that He wants to intervene in this situation/person's life. (See Heb 11:6; Rom 14:23b.)

- Be careful not to dictate to God what should be done in this situation. It is all right to express your desires and opinions, but *do not* tell Him how to answer your prayer. Trust Him for knowing the best solution. (See Rom 8:28.)

- Recognize that you are dealing with a powerful enemy and that you must not come against him in your own strength but rather in the power and name of Jesus.

- Empathize with those for whom you are praying.

- Follow scriptural prayer examples as you intercede. David gives many good examples in the psalms of bringing daily concerns to the Lord in prayer for Him to solve. He shows how to look at circumstances and then look to the great and powerful God who is able to help you overcome the circumstance or to change it for your good. Paul also shows you that you need to pray specifically for the deepening and development of the spiritual character of those you love rather than always focusing on circumstances surrounding their lives. (See Eph. 1:18–20; 3:14–19; Phil. 1:9–11; Col. 1:9–12.) Your desire in prayer for others (as well as yourself) should be that your character is developed so that you will be "perfect and complete, lacking in nothing" (Jas 1:4).

Example of adapting Colossians 1:9–10:

Father, Please fill George with the knowledge of Your will in all spiritual wisdom and understanding, so that he may walk in a manner worthy of our Lord, to please You in all respects. I pray that George may bear fruit in every good work and increase in the knowledge of You.

Praying Scripture to the Lord

One of the more powerful forms of prayer is to take scriptural commands, promises, or principles that are specifically for you today and pray them back to the Lord. In this way you know you are praying according to His will and that He will answer (1 John 5:13–14).

This can be done in several ways, three of which are mentioned here with samples.

This would be easy to do during your quiet time when you come across a verse that is meaningful to you. For example, when you read Psalm 55:22, "Cast your cares on the Lord and he will sustain you; He will never let the righteous fall," you may want to pray:

Pray Specific Verse to God

> Lord, Help me to always give You all my problems and cares. Please remind me to do so whenever problems come. Are there any problems or cares I need to turn over to You right now that I've been holding on to? Thank you that you do sustain me and will not let me fall. Many times I have seen You do this. What a good God You are!

You will find that the prayers of Paul in Ephesians 1:17–19, Philippians 1:9–11, Colossians 1:9–12, and of others, and David in Psalms are excellent.

Pray Passage of Scripture

An example of this could be from Psalm 103. Read verse 1, "Bless the Lord, O my soul: and all that is within me, bless His holy name"(NASB). Then pray:

> Father, I do bless Your Holy name. You are worthy of all praise and honor. Thank You for sending Jesus Christ to be my Lord and Savior.

Then read verse 2, "Bless the Lord, O my soul, and forget none of His benefits (NASB). Pray:

> Thank You, Lord, for all the blessings You give to Your children. How I thank You for the privilege of coming to You in prayer at any time. Thank You for letting me live in a land where I am free to worship You. Please be with those who love You and do not have such a privilege. Encourage them and strengthen them to be able to withstand all the pressures that are put on them to compromise their faith. Please meet their daily needs as You've promised You will.

Continue on until you get to the end of the psalm.

Pray Theme Scriptures This type of praying is very appropriate when you have an ongoing concern or often find yourself praying for the type of request in the theme. This might focus on such topics as finances, fear, desirable character qualities, salvation, or troubles. You will need to do a little scriptural research to find appropriate verses and link them together in prayer. A concordance or *Nave's Topical Bible* is very helpful in finding the best verses. Write them all out, and put them together in a logical sequence to use in intercession. (See examples in resources 16I, J, K.)

How to Pray
For Family Members

A Husband's Prayers for His Wife

Pray that she will:

- Have patience—with children, in doing routine chores, etc.
- Enjoy her day and her children.
- Have the joy of the Lord.
- Have enough time to do all her work.
- Have a meaningful quiet time and will develop a close relationship with the Lord.
- Spend her money wisely.
- Be a good witness and testimony to her neighbors.
- Feel fulfilled in her role as mother and wife.
- Be able to use Biblical principles in dealing with the children.
- Get enough rest and stay healthy.
- Know what to do when emergencies come.
- Be protected at all times.
- Recognize the enemy's attacks such as worry, discouragement, fear, or anger, and will resist them.

A Wife's Prayers for Her Husband

Pray that he will:

- Do his job well, accurately.
- Look to God for guidance in all decisions.
- Find favor with his colleagues, bosses.
- Be ethical, honest.

- Be a good witness to all he works with, including those who come to his business for services such as sales persons or that he may contact if he is in sales.
- Be known as a godly man.
- Enjoy his work, even in the difficult times.

Also ask the Lord to help your husband to :

- Have a right balance between God, work, and family.
- Be the spiritual leader of the family.
- Be protected from any type of temptation, including sexual, monetary, or undue desire for power.
- Be totally aware of all his gifts from the Lord and will use them as God directs.
- Walk moment by moment under God's control in every area of his life.

For any weaknesses that are present, find positive Scriptures to pray for strengthening your spouse and he or she overcoming the problem through God's strength and power. You may have to pray that God will make the person aware of and willing to let the Lord correct the problem.

In addition to the specific prayer time set aside each day, husbands and wives can pray for family members every time they see their pictures on their desks, in their wallets, or at home. They can also pray while doing housework, on hold on the phone, when waiting for someone for an appointment, standing in line, at lunch, driving to work, in the shower, while dressing, or during commercials on TV.

Prayers for Children

Pray that they will:

- Accept the spiritual guidance of parents and the church.
- Have a hunger for the Word and will memorize it and meditate on it.
- Choose godly companions and be protected from any child who might lead them astray or wrongly influence their thinking.
- Be protected from wrong thinking.
- Avoid even the appearance of evil.
- Avoid all temptations.
- Have wisdom in all they do.
- Learn easily and do well in their studies.
- Be obedient and desire to do right.

- Have godly character qualities as found in Philippians 1:9–11; Ephesians 3:16–19, and 2 Timothy 1:7.

Prayers for Teenagers

Pray that they will:

- Want to have godly principles and standards.
- Resist peer temptations.
- Resist all temptations—especially drugs, sex, pornography, and bad movies/videos.
- Accept the guidance of their parents and respect their counsel and standards.
- Develop the sensitivity to see the needs of others, have a desire to help others and care about them, and then do whatever they can to reach out to others.
- Seek the Lord for their future.
- Let God prepare them to be a good spouse.
- Trust God to prepare their future spouse to be a godly person and mate.
- Have godly character qualities as found in Philippians 1:9–11; Ephesians 3:16–19, and 2 Timothy 1:7.

For any weaknesses that are present, find positive Scriptures to pray for strengthening your children and teenagers and their overcoming of problems through God's strength and power. You may have to pray that God will make them aware of and willing to let the Lord correct this problem.

Prayers for the Family as a Whole

Pray that your family will:

- Be godly and led by God, with each member walking closely with the Lord.
- Have real unity and love between each and every member.
- Be a good Christian testimony to everyone around.

Prayer for Character Qualities

Father,

Cause _____ to be filled with the full, deep and clear knowledge of Your will. May _____ have a comprehensive insight into Your ways and purposes and have an understanding and discernment of spiritual things.

May _____ walk in a manner worthy of You and be fully pleasing to You. May _____ desire to please You in all things and bear fruit in every good work. May _____ steadily grow and increase in the knowledge of You, having a fuller, deeper and clearer insight and recognition of and acquaintance with You.

May _____ be invigorated and strengthened with all power, according to the might of Your glory. May _____ exercise every kind of endurance, patience, perseverance and forbearing and do it all with joy. May _____ be well-grounded and settled and steadfast in _____ faith, not shifting or moving away from hope in You. May _____'s love abound more and more and extend to its fullest development in knowledge and keen insight. May _____ love display itself in greater depth of acquaintance and more comprehensive discernment. May _____ learn to sense what is vital and approve and prize what is excellent and of real value, recognizing the highest and best and distinguishing the moral differences. May _____ be pure, unerring and blameless with a sincere and certain heart.

May _____ not do anything to cause others to stumble. May _____ abound in and be filled with the fruits of righteousness. May _____ be strengthened and reinforced with mighty power in _____ inner person by the Holy Spirit. Make Your home, Lord Jesus in _____'s heart.

May _____ be rooted deep in love and founded securely on love. May _____ have the power and be strong to apprehend and grasp and understand what is the breadth, length, height, and depth of Your love. May _____ be filled with Your fullness, being flooded with You. May _____ not have a spirit of fear, timidity, or cowardice but rather a spirit of power and love and a calm, well-balanced mind. May _____ be disciplined and self-controlled.

(Prayer based on the *Amplified Bible:* Col. 1:9–12,23; Phil. 1:9–11; Eph. 3:16–19; 2 Tim. 1:7.)

Prayer About Trials, Troubles, or Temptations

Loving Father,

Help _____ during this difficult time. Help _____ give You all cares, anxieties, worries, and concerns once and for all. Let _____ know You care and are always watchful. Encourage _____ and let _____ know You never let the righteous fall.

May _____ be reassured and confident that all things in life are working out for the very best and that if You are for _____ there is no one who can succeed against _____, including Satan. Remind _____ that no weapon designed to hurt _____ can succeed and that You will vindicate. Reassure _____ that You will liberally supply ALL needs according to Your own unlimited riches. Help _____ to walk by faith, not by sight or appearance. Let _____ have no unbelief or distrust nor allow _____ to waver or doubtingly question you concerning Your promises.

Let _____ grow strong and be empowered by faith. Let _____ be full of joy, exulting and triumphant in troubles and rejoicing in sufferings. Let _____ be convinced and know that pressure and affliction and hardship are producing patience and unswerving endurance in _____, and that these will produce maturity of character with approved faith and tried integrity. Remind _____ to ask for wisdom throughout this trial.

May _____ look to You as _____ rock. Please reassure _____ that "weeping may remain for a night, but rejoicing comes in the morning"; for "after [_____ has] suffered a little while, the God of all grace—Who imparts all blessing and favor—has called _____ to His [own] eternal glory in Christ Jesus will Himself complete and make _____ what _____ ought to be, establish and ground _____ securely, and strengthen _____. Help _____ believe that indeed _____ has the strength to do all things through Your empowering.

May _____ be ready for anything and equal to anything through You who infuses inner strength into _____ . Let _____ be self-sufficient in Christ's sufficiency. Help _____ to endure hardships and sufferings, remembering that You will instruct, counsel, and watch over _____. May You, the God of peace, give Your peace that goes far beyond our human understanding and help _____ to be tranquil and fear nothing from You and be content with _____ earthly lot.

(Prayer is based on Amplified verses, unless otherwise noted, from 1 Pet. 5:7; Ps. 55:22; Rom. 8:28,31; Isa. 54:17; Phil. 4:19; 2 Cor. 5:7; Rom. 4:20,21; 5:3,4; Jas. 1:2-6; Ps. 18:2; 30:5 (NIV); 1 Pet. 5:10; Phil. 4:13; 2 Tim. 2:3; Ps. 25:12 (NIV); 32:8; 1 Thess. 5:23.)

Prayer for a Difficult Person

Pray this prayer for yourself first so this is not used as a prayer "club" to attack the person.

Loving Father,

Cause _____ to "(lead a life) worthy of the [divine] calling to which You have called _____—with behavior that is a credit to the summons to [Your] service, living as becomes _____—with complete humility, meekness, and patience, bearing with one another and making allowances because [we] love one another. May _____ be eager to strive earnestly to guard and keep the harmony produced by Your Spirit in the binding power of peace. May _____ act in a way that shows there is one body. May _____ be perfected and fully equipped by You. May _____'s love be agape love that endures long and is patient and kind. May _____ not be rude nor unmannerly or act unbecomingly.

Help _____ not to insist on _____'s own rights or _____'s own way. May _____ not be self-seeking, touchy or fretful or resentful. May _____ take no account of evil done, or dwell on a suffered wrong. Help _____ bear up under whatever may happen without weakening, to always look for the best in every person. May _____'s hopes be fadeless under all circumstances. May _____ love never fail.

May _____'s love abound more and more in knowledge and depth of insight, so that _____ may be able to discern what is best and may be free and blameless until the day of Christ, filled with the fruit of righteousness that comes through Jesus Christ—to the glory and praise of God.

How to Pray For the Sick

Remember God is in control. (See Rom. 8:28, 1 Thess. 5:18.)

Seek God's wisdom for:
- How to pray for this condition.
- Physicians diagnosis and treatment.
- Determining if this condition was a result of lifestyle or sin.

Ask God for:
- His will to be done.
- His name to be glorified during this time.
- Healing of the condition. (See Ps. 103:3.)
- Those who are sick to be sustained. (See Ps. 41:3.)
- Restoration of health. (See Ps. 41:3.)
- Our acceptance of a prolonged condition, should God allow this to happen. (See Isa. 55:8,9; 2 Cor.12:7–10.)

Involve others to pray by faith for restoration. (See Jas. 5:14,15.)

Trust God for the outcome of:
- Perseverance.
- Character.
- Endurance.
- Completeness.
- A good testimony to others. (See Rom. 5:3–5; Jas. 1:2–5.)

How to Pray Through a Song

There are several ways you can use songs to enhance your prayer time, your worship of the Lord. Besides the obvious of singing them, or listening to them played, is that of using the words of a song to stimulate your praying. This can be used every day, especially with different Christian holiday music such as Christmas. Remember, these words are appropriate to use at any time of the year. The following are two brief examples of how to pray through a song, phrase by phrase. Don't feel you have to do every word/phrase or even verse if nothing comes to your mind for prayer. These are only tools to help enrich your prayer time.

Holy, Holy, Holy

Holy, holy, holy!
Lord God Almighty!

- Acknowledge the holiness of God, that He is worthy to be worshipped and praised.
- Confirm that He is your Lord and your God, and that you submit to His lordship in every area of your life.
- Agree that He has all power. For example, you might pray, "Lord, You are absolutely holy. There is no sin in You at all. You are the only God, Lord of all, and have all power."

Early in the morning our song shall rise to thee.

- In prayer, commit to prayer and singing to the Lord in the morning. Consider doing this as the first thing of your day.

Merciful and mighty!

- Express your gratitude to Him for His many mercies you've experienced. Name some of them specifically.

- Acknowledge His might, rulership, and absolute control over the world.

God in three Persons, Blessed Trinity!

- Acknowledge that the Lord is Triune. Thank each one of the Trinity for their role and help in your life.
- Bless Him for His Being.

Joy to the world! the Lord is come.   Joy to the World

- Express the joy you have because Jesus came and the meaning of His coming to the world.

  For example, you might pray:

  Father, Thank you so much for sending Jesus into the world to be born here, live here as our example, and die for our sins. What joy fills my heart when I think of all His coming means to me in my life. My salvation, the guidance You give me, my eternal life with You and all You are doing in me to make me more like Jesus.

Let earth receive her King.

  You might pray:

  Lord, Jesus, I receive You as my King. Live in my life in all I do. I want to be submissive to You in all I do. Show me any time I am not letting You be King of my life.

Let every heart prepare Him room.

  You could pray for the salvation of relatives and other unbelievers, that they will have their heart prepared to receive Jesus into their life.

And Heaven and nature sing.

- Agree to the fact that there is rejoicing in heaven over our lost ones coming to Him.
- You can tell the Lord that You want to join with all creation in singing because of the coming of Jesus into the world.

Prayer Partners Covenant

I will pray regularly for the things we share in prayer. I further covenant with _____ that I will not speak of the things we share for prayer with anyone else. Anything we discuss in our relationship as prayer partners will be held in the strictest confidence.

Signed: _____